A Waterloo Hero

Publishing note

The original German edition was published in Hamelin in 1846, under the title of *Erinnerungen eines Soldaten aus den Feldzügen der Königlich-deutschen Legion (Reminiscences of a soldier from the campaigns of the King's German Legion)*, with a foreword by Franz Georg Ferdinand Schläger. Now published for the first time in English, this edition includes a new introduction by the translator, James Bogle, and explanatory passages by Andrew Uffindell. The chapter headings, subheadings, maps and notes have also been added.

A WATERLOO HERO
THE REMINISCENCES OF FRIEDRICH LINDAU

BY
FRIEDRICH LINDAU

Former Rifleman of the 2nd Light Battalion
Holder of the Guelphic Medal, the Waterloo Medal
and the Bronze Medal of Merit

Foreword by Franz Georg Ferdinand Schläger

Translated, Edited and Presented by
James Bogle and Andrew Uffindell

Frontline Books, London

A Waterloo Hero: The Reminiscences of Friedrich Lindau

This edition published in 2009 by Frontline Books, an imprint of Pen &
Sword Books Limited, 47 Church Street, Barnsley, S. Yorkshire, S70 2AS
www.frontline-books.com

ISBN: 978-1-84832-539-5

The Publisher would like to thank Gareth Glover for his support in the
production of this book.

A CIP data record for this title is available from the British Library.

For more information on our books, please visit
www.frontline-books.com, email info@frontline-books.com
or write to us at the above address.

Typeset by JCS Publishing Services Ltd, www.jcs-publishing.co.uk

Maps drawn by Red Lion Prints

Printed in the UK by the MPG Books Group

CONTENTS

Maps

Translator's Introduction

The circumstances that led me to make this translation of Friedrich Lindau's 'Reminiscences' are rather unusual. I knew from my family records that my great-great-grandfather, Jacob Ole Lindam [sic], who was born a Dane, had served as a young officer in the King's German Legion for the greater part of the Peninsular War and at Waterloo under the command of the Duke of Wellington. I wished to research the role of the Legion in this campaign and I was led by the British Library catalogue to a book published in German in 1846, the reminiscences of a private soldier in the 2nd Light Infantry Battalion of the Legion. I knew that Ole Lindam (as he was generally known) also served in this battalion. When I began to translate I found a very telling vivid narrative, so in the course of time I grew familiar with the whole book. It was with considerable pleasure that I found out that Ole Lindam was Lindau's company commander (No 1 Company, 2nd Light Infantry Battalion, King's German Legion) and that he was twice mentioned by name in the narrative and may have been referred to on other occasions simply as 'my captain'. So I have a personal connection with the book.

Lindau's 'Reminiscences' is one of the very few accounts of the Peninsular Campaign given by a private soldier in the King's German Legion. The narrative was presented without any breaks (the chapter headings and subheadings are added). Lindau's memories were recorded with the help of a pastor, Rector Hansen. Lindau was illiterate and so his 'Reminiscences' were dictated. Although there were thirty years or more between the events recorded and the publication of the book Lindau generally seems to have had a very good memory of the happenings he witnessed, though there are a few minor discrepancies, and his narrative tallies well with the standard history of the King's German Legion by North Ludlow Beamish and also with the account of his commanding officer at the defence of the farmstead of La Haye Sainte at Waterloo, Major George Baring, who singled out Lindau for his courage – the only private soldier that he mentioned. One may suppose that the ordinary soldiers had little idea of the campaign as a whole. Rather plaintively Lindau remarked of the retreat from Burgos in 1812:

> I was made angry that we continuously had to fall back before the enemy, who could well think that we were afraid of them, which was by no means the case. If it had depended on our battalion we would not have let ourselves be driven back even one foot by the whole of the French army, but the commands of the superiors must be obeyed by the soldier even if against his will.

Friedrich Lindau was christened Georg Friedrich Wilhelm at Hamelin Garrison Church on 19 January 1788. His father, August Wilhelm Valentin, served as a soldier in the Hanoverian service for twenty-three years as a lance-corporal; on discharge from the army he worked as a weaver. He was a strict disciplinarian. Two of Friedrich's godfathers were also soldiers. His mother, Hanne Christiane Sophie Rudolph also came from Hamelin. Friedrich had five sisters and two brothers: the older brother, Georg Ludwig, born in 1789, served in the King's German Legion like Friedrich, but as a butcher; and the younger, Christian Wilhelm, born in 1792, served in the Legion as an artilleryman.

As a youth Friedrich was confirmed before being put as an apprentice to a shoemaker, his lifetime's trade, but as his master treated him harshly he ran away. Another master took him on as a shoemaker, but mostly employed him on other business so that even after leaving the army he still had to complete his training for his trade. Friedrich long desired to go to England to join the army and finally ran away from home on Martin's Day, 4 July 1809. He was hotly pursued by his brother Christian, who had to be forcibly deterred from coming too, though he was able to join up later. After an adventurous journey Lindau arrived in Harwich on 27 July. He marched with other recruits to the Unattached Recruits Depot at Lymington, then on 5 August marched to Bexhill where he arrived on the 17th. He was formally enlisted on 24 August to join the 1st Company of the 2nd Light Infantry Battalion of the King's German Legion as a rifleman (private soldier); he signed on for seven years and received his bounty of four guineas. His description on recruitment was blue eyes, blond hair, fair complexion and height 5' 7" (his discharge papers gave his height as 5' 9").

The years of Lindau's service are fully covered in the narrative.

Lindau's name was included in the Muster Roll of those who served at the Battle of Waterloo and in due course he was awarded the Waterloo Medal; he was also awarded the Guelphic Medal, a tribute to his courage at the Siege of San Sebastian and in the defence of La Haye Sainte at Waterloo. He obtained his discharge from the army from his commanding officer George Baring (by then a lieutenant-colonel) on 24 October 1815 at the Bois de Boulogne in Paris. His papers noted that he had served for eight years and two months; he actually served for six years and two months – Waterloo counted for an extra two years of service. The discharge paper records that he was severely wounded at Vitoria and Waterloo. The Guelphic Medal carried a pension and in addition in 1820 he was recommended for a pension from the Royal Hospital Chelsea in respect of the wound to his right arm at the Battle of Vitoria.

After his return to Hamelin Lindau resumed his work as a shoemaker and married. His wife died in 1827 but he married a second time. By 1846, when the 'Reminiscences' were published and Schläger wrote his foreword, there is a strong suggestion that Lindau had fallen on hard times. Schläger draws attention to Lindau's nine children, of which four were still at school – mouths to feed. Were it not for his pensions he would have very little income for his business was not prospering. Doubtless one of the reasons for the publication of the 'Reminiscences' was to afford him some financial relief. In 1849 Lindau received the (English) Military General Service Medal (Peninsular War Medal), which he signed for; Lindau qualified for six clasps: Albuera, Salamanca, Vitoria, San Sebastian,

Nivelle and Nive. In 1865 a list was made of soldiers in Hamelin still alive who had fought in the years 1813–15; Lindau's name does not appear among them, so it must be taken that by then he had died.

Friedrich Lindau was a courageous man.

James Bogle

FOREWORD

Over thirty years have now passed since Napoleon was forced to lay down his bloody sword. Lindau has contributed honestly and truly according to his ability to what the King's German Legion did in the years from 1811 to 1815 for their conquest of Spain, France and the Netherlands. Now, after a generation has passed, many of his valiant comrades in arms have been laid to rest and most of the others have grey hair. He has resolved to travel that hard road once again in spirit to snatch his experiences from oblivion. For this purpose he found Rector Hansen a friendly support who, for many evenings, often till midnight, took down the stories of the military adventure and thus brought the reminiscences to the form in which they now lie before us. These unpretentious pages, without exaggeration and without affectation, comprise what Lindau experienced, endured and what he saw of the greater happenings that the history books would make known to later generations. He offers this to his comrades in arms in the hope that it will refresh some memories in them, and also with the wish that forgiveness might be found for how rash blood in its recklessness – often in great need – offended the law of war and love of one's neighbour. It is indeed an old principle: '*inter arma silent leges*' – in war laws fall silent – and the honest frankness with which Lindau concealed nothing at all, apart from where he allows himself discretion, is favourable proof that he tells the truth. It must be agreeable for everyone who enjoys reading about campaigns to listen for once to a man for whom cultivated thought is lacking and who looks at many things with quite different eyes, as the educated suppress, taking much to be erroneous and passing over it, much too to be improper and unlawful. Works such as this properly enable us to cast a clear glance at the life of a military expedition and to appreciate and to experience the sufferings, the adversities and the misery, and to come to know what the soldier and his superiors experience in war.

Truly one cannot be grateful enough to the heroes who offer as a sacrifice their arms, their health and their lives for the freedom and the good of their native land. I always have wished that in every land he who is exhausted by exertions and is incapable of any work – often a soldier robbed of his eyes, his arms or his legs – might have such a refuge as is offered in Paris at the Invalides, where they spend the twilight of their days in peace, mutually in the honour they won, and through which costly support for the soldiers can ease their wounds and pains from their experiences. This appears to be some recompense, as far as recompense is possible, for the grey-haired man who has been in the wars – it is not enough to protect him from need in his old age, and it moves me if a disabled man in torn clothes asks for a gift to ease his hunger. One should also reflect how one openly expresses one's thankfulness to the defender of the native land, and rather than found an institution that receives and cares as a cloister for the handicapped, one might spend a significant sum for the erection of monuments and victory columns. One can do the one, without leaving out the other. The valiant soldier is worth such a refuge.

In England there is such an institution for super-annuated soldiers, and the pensions that are disbursed to pensioners there are magnificent. In our own native land pensions are also paid from the King's Majesty, from his Royal Highness the Crown Prince, from the War Ministry, from the society for the aid of widows and orphans and from those of goodwill. Many anxieties about afflictions are thus lifted, but all of this is not enough to repay the enduring powerful work of the invalid. Praise God that through the circumstances of a new age the number of handicapped people is decreasing and that the care for this smaller number of people can be more effective. The old die off gradually. Certainly everyone who reads Lindau's 'Reminiscences' and considers the privations and the exertions that the army in Spain were subjected to will agree with the wishes that I express. Whoever considers the horror that such a war brings with it will be glad that wars must become ever rarer among civilised people, that disputes will be debated with the pen in the cabinet rather than with swords on the battlefield, and done away with. Large standing armies – which are an enormous burden for every country – will be ever less necessary for the future. If danger threatens then everyone, youngster and grown man, will rekindle their desire to protect the throne and the native land, like our Lindau who gladly left his native town to follow his king's calling and to oppose the common enemy.

Lindau was born on 19 January 1788 in Hamelin, where his father was a weaver. From an early age he was accustomed to being obedient through his father's strictness, and kept away from certain dangers. He grew up and after his confirmation was apprenticed to a shoemaker, but ran away when he could no longer put up with his harsh treatment, and found another master who made demands on him beyond the intended trade. As he was not thoroughly knowledgeable, when Lindau wanted to become a partner and later, when he returned from the campaign, he had to learn the basics of the trade again and fill in the gaps in his training. Now for thirty years he has been a master shoemaker who understands his subject excellently. Nineteen years ago he lost his wife and married for the second time. Nine of his children are alive, of which four youngsters go to school. As all trades have been very much depressed through great competition so his business suffers, and would founder, even though his fine wife stands by him and helps, if he did not get the English pension of some fifty thalers and the connected support from the Guelphic Medal of twenty-seven thalers ten standard silver groschen.

Lindau is – as Major-General Baron von Baring* also has written to me – 'a straight, upright man', who is distinguished through his presence of mind, through his fearlessness in the face of danger, through his loyalty to his superiors, through his distinguished good nature and who enjoys the love of all his comrades. He is the same man of whom N. Ludlow Beamish makes mention in his *History*

---

* As Major George Baring had by then become.

of the King's German Legion: 'one of the most excellent of this present time' – at the defence of La Haye Sainte on 18 June 1815. He said 'There was a skirmisher of the 2nd Light Battalion, by the name of Friedrich Lindau, who, although bleeding heavily from two head wounds nevertheless stubbornly kept to his post at the little barn door from where he defended the main entrance. Major Baring saw that the light bandage on his wounds did not staunch the flow of blood sufficiently and ordered him again to go back. In spite of his wounds and a rich purse of plundered gold that he kept by him, his resolute and simple answer was: "Only a scoundrel could leave his officer while his head still remains on his shoulders." This courageous soldier was later taken prisoner and lost his purse of gold.'

That Lindau in his 'Reminiscences' thought less on the overall plan of the campaign and the large-scale result of it than on the particulars he himself saw and experienced, lay in his natural circumstances; it was not granted to a man in his position to survey the whole picture. Nevertheless there are enough writings that pass on information Lindau was not able to tell. But one can come to know how carefully he paid attention to everything and how hard he dug into some of the disagreeable things in his memories if one compares his account of the Battle of Waterloo with the account of Major-General Baron von Baring. Should anyone be surprised that I am introducing these 'Reminiscences' into the world, I must only say as my apology that Lindau is a citizen of the town of Hamelin and a member of my parish, whose welfare lies very close to my heart and whose outward circumstances I gladly feel committed perhaps to improve in this way. And should the purpose of these 'Reminiscences' be attained I would ask that it be credited not to me, but to Rector Hansen, who put the 'Reminiscences' in order with much care and kept firmly in view the level of education of the narrator. The public should also be grateful to him that this book has not been rejected. I have only lightened the printing and publication of it according to my capacity in order to enrich the crown of valour, which is due to him.

Franz Georg Ferdinand Schläger
Hamelin, 26 May 1846

1

ESCAPE TO ENGLAND
1806–1811

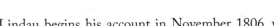

Lindau begins his account in November 1806, when he was a teenager living in the town of Hamelin, in the north German state of Hanover.

Ever since 1714, when the Elector of Hanover had become King George I of Britain, the two countries had shared the same ruler, while remaining separate states. But Hanover, unlike Britain, was exposed on the mainland, and sandwiched between the stronger powers of France and Prussia. When the short-lived Peace of Amiens between Britain and France collapsed in May 1803, Napoleon ordered General Edouard Mortier to occupy Hanover with a French army. Two years later, in 1805, he offered the territory to Prussia, to induce her to remain neutral while he crushed the Austrian and Russian armies during the Austerlitz campaign.

Prussia duly acquired Hanover, but grew increasingly alarmed at Napoleon's growing power. The threat was starkly underlined in July 1806, when he grouped his German satellite states into a powerful bloc known as the Confederation of the Rhine, and thereby replaced Austria as the dominant power in central Europe. On

1 October, the Prussian King, Friedrich Wilhelm III, issued an ultimatum for all French forces to withdraw over the Rhine, and war immediately followed.

The result was a disaster for Prussia. Thrusting north-eastwards from southern Germany towards Berlin, Napoleon smashed the Prussian armies at the twin battles of Jena and Auerstädt. He then exploited his victory with one of the most relentless and successful pursuits in military history, completing the destruction of the Prussian army and causing a whole series of fortresses to capitulate with minimal resistance.

One of these strongholds was Hamelin, whose commandant, Major-General von Schöler, was seventy-five years old. The town was occupied not by the Grande Armée under Napoleon's direct command, but by a detached corps of French and Dutch troops under Mortier, which advanced to take control of Hanover from the south-west. Hamelin was protected by such strong fortifications that it was known as the 'Gibraltar of the North', and its Prussian garrison actually outnumbered the forces brought against it, yet it surrendered without a fight on 20 November. As Lindau describes, the news of the capitulation destroyed the discipline of the Prussian troops, and caused widespread drunkenness and disorder.

The fortifications of Hamelin were subsequently demolished. Much of Hanover was incorporated into one of Napoleon's newly created satellite states, the Kingdom of Westphalia, while the northern part was directly annexed by the French Empire. Only in 1813 would Hanover be liberated, as Napoleon's power collapsed.

North Sea

KINGDOM
OF
DENMARK

SWEDEN

Baltic Sea

Heligoland

MECKLENBURG
SCHWERIN

KINGDOM
OF
HOLLAND

Bremen

P R U S S I A

AMSTERDAM

Hanover

Hamelin

BERLIN

BRUSSELS

S A X O N Y

Auerstädt

Jena

Dresden

PRAGUE

Luxembourg

AUSTRIAN

FRENCH

CONFEDERATION

EMPIRE

Stuttgart

EMPIRE

Strasbourg

Augsburg

Munich

OF THE

Salzburg

RHINE

N

BERN

W   E

HELVETIA

S

Geneva

VALAIS

Milan

K I N G D O M

Venice

O F

I T A L Y

Genoa

Adriatic Sea

0   100 m

0   100 km

CENTRAL EUROPE, 1806

'A TERRIBLE NIGHT'

The night that preceded the day on which the town was surrendered to the French was terrible for the inhabitants of Hamelin. As the rumour spread that the commanding officer had capitulated and that the soldiers, separated from their officers, would be taken to France as prisoners of war, so they met full of bitterness and, without the orders of their superiors to obey, broke open the magazine on 20 November 1806 when it was dark. Soon after, masses of soldiers drunk on rum and wine marched with their weapons through the streets, shot into the windows and wounded each other. Others brought powder barrels on to the streets to blow the town into the air. The crowd, brought to desperation, uttering curses, surged towards the residence of the commandant, Major-General von Schöler, and certainly would have taken dreadful revenge on him for the betrayal had not the cavalry protected his house from the frenzied people.

While in this manner the storm of a liberated war-like horde raged on the streets of my home town, it was impossible for me to stay in the quiet little room of my parents, where my anxious father trembled before the terrible call of 'Fire!' and my mother with clasped hands called on heaven for help. I wanted to see what was happening outside; the desire for loot also attracted me. My parents begged me to stay with them and not to risk my life so carelessly; but in vain. I slunk up to the door, through the uproar on the streets and came to the Osterthor, where in the casemate I found a drunken Prussian soldier who didn't stop me from scooping up a bucketful of rum with which, I, protected by the dark, fortunately arrived back in front of our house. Meanwhile, in front of the house of our neighbours, where a captain had his quarters, his company assembled and was now just on the point of storming our house, from which some shots had fallen on the ranks. Someone shot through the closed shutters, wounded an old woman in the shoulder and killed a Prussian soldier who was in the lower room. The door of the house was broken; I came with a crowd into the house; someone stormed up the stairs and dragged my father out of the room since he was taken to be the originator of the shot. However, he succeeded in diverting the anger of the soldiers by protesting his innocence. They broke into another room that was barricaded; here they found some soldiers with rifles that had just been discharged. In his anger, the captain wanted to bayonet one of them, but the wife of the threatened man fell down, grasped the knee of the furious man and saved the life of her husband. However, she could not prevent the suspicious men striking him with a rifle butt and dragging the man to the guardhouse.

When it was quiet again in the house, I carried on; I wandered around the streets and watched the activity of the soldiers; here some of them who were no longer able to roll a barrel of rum swore; there a soldier fumed at a closed door and demanded that the householder buy a cask of rice; others smashed their weapons so that they did not fall intact into the hands of the hated French. Meanwhile I managed to collect eight undamaged rifles, fine polished weapons, for which I was heartily glad. I hurried home with them and hid them under a pile of

17

roof tiles that lay in the yard. Then I ventured out again, it might have been about four o'clock in the morning, and I reached Bäckerstrasse, where my brother-in-law lived. All at once a crowd of Prussian soldiers stormed his house and demanded that he should buy what they offered for sale. I came soon enough to be able to help him. As he had made up his mind to refuse to comply with the soldiers' demands, one of them hit him with his bayonet. That was too much for us; we seized a pitchfork and forced the soldiers out of the house.

Meanwhile we met a peaceable man opposite. The householder bought from a Prussian soldier a large cask of raisins for a thaler. Next I hurried to the Münsterkirchhof to see what was developing, only in Kirchstrasse there was a mass of people coming towards me, fleeing on foot, with the cavalry strongly attacking them in order to bring them back to order and halt further excesses. Here the shooting was so bad that I preferred to run back very quickly and seek shelter in my brother-in-law's house, which I had just left, and where I remained until daybreak. Then the storm died down; most of the soldiers had escaped from the Osterthor in the darkness of the night in order to avoid wretched imprisonment; only individual drunken ones wandered round here and there on the street.

About ten o'clock in the morning the first Dutchmen and Frenchmen advanced into the Neuethor. I had to see them, so much did I hate the enemy who had succeeded in opening the entrance to my native town with gold. Near the gate at the corner of Ritterstrasse four Prussian soldiers had taken post and shot at the advancing enemy with drunken courage. But immediately a Dutch cavalryman rode out towards them, split the head of one of them and chased the remainder, who threw away their rifles in their flight. Now all the inhabitants fled their houses, so I hurried out and went to the nearest barracks, so that, if I found anything of value, it might evade the hands of the hated enemy. Here I saw everything in pieces; in the meantime I collected a leather pack and luckily reached home with it, having made my way through gardens and courtyards; there my parents were glad to have me safe and sound with them again.

Though it pleased me very little I had to remain in the house, since the enemy had made it known that no one should be seen on the street, under penalty of death. In this way two days passed in which the French established themselves in Hamelin.

People were then sought to undertake the care of the wounded and sick. Since in these turbulent days my father's trade* could not continue, he registered and was employed, together with me and my mother. This service, often heartbreaking, we performed for about half a year in which each of us earned seven thaler a month and in which we had a great deal of work and no rest day or night. The schoolhouse, which had formerly served as a dwelling house for the canons of the Monastery of San Bonifacii, was furnished as a military hospital and completely filled with wounded Prussians and French.

One of these men aroused my particular sympathy. He was a very young man from the neighbourhood of the province of Minden, who had a bullet in his leg. He

---

* Lindau senior was a weaver.

constantly grieved for his father and mother, whom it seemed certain he would not see alive again, and lamented his and his parents' lot. But the young man's parents yearned for their child and had come to Hamelin with a carriage. They turned to me for they knew that their son lay in hospital and implored me that I might get their child so that they could take him home with them.

I promised my help, called the father in the evening to get the carriage ready in front of the lodging and himself to appear at the corner of the Münsterkirche; I wanted then to see what would be possible. Trusting in the goodwill that the doctor of the hospital always showed to me, since I was always at hand in a friendly way, I risked it, as darkness was approaching, by taking the young Prussian on my back. I lied to the guard that I wanted to convey the sick man to the doctor in the bath and he let me through unhindered. With beating heart the father waited for me at the Münsterkirche, took away the load that was so dear to him and presented me with a thaler. We took turns to carry the sick man to the carriage that stopped outside the Zur Stadt Hamburg Inn where the mother received us with tears of joy. I accompanied the carriage all the way to the Neuethor where the gateway clerk, whom I knew well, let us pass freely after I had let him into the secret; then I returned to the hospital with a light heart. The next morning the Prussian was missing and a commission organised to investigate; I ought to know where he was. I thought it proper, however, only to declare that I had seen him stand up yesterday evening with the help of his crutch. After the commission had left I told the doctor the whole story, which pleased him; he was glad that the young man had found his parents again, having pined for them so often.

Certainly in the hospital the wounded were well looked after, but some of them wanted to have tobacco, which was not to be had. In order to provide it I brought some pieces of wood into the town to sell to the large wood store that lay on the Münsterkirchhof. I was accompanied by an old man, a lightly wounded Prussian who waited at table, and I bought tobacco with the money raised from the wood and slipped it to the wounded Prussian. He was granted such refreshment because, besides the pain of his wounds, he had to put up with the disdain of the Dutchmen and the French and all the horrors of the hospital. Here lay an unconscious dying man who was making his death rattle; there another commended himself to the Lord with fervent prayer and breathed his last with the last words of his prayer. Here was a dying man who in his unspeakable pains cursed the hour of his birth and gave up his soul with shouts and screams. With such scenes I now had to pass my days and my nights, to give medicine for one, to pour out tea for another, to try to restrain a third in bed if he wanted to get up in the fever of his wounds. One evening I was so tired and exhausted that instead of going to bed I lay beside a wounded man, without noticing it. I was woken up in the night by one of the sick men who wanted to have some tea. On waking up I felt something cold by my side – I lay beside a corpse. Nearly every night six or seven of these unfortunate men died and were removed in the morning; if it were a Prussian he would be thrown down the stairs by the brutal French. The dead were laid out in a little room by the kitchen until the doctor came

21

to cut the body in two, put it in a coffin and send it on to the churchyard, from where the coffin would be brought back to the hospital each time to receive the new offering of death.

From this place of misery a commissary rescued me; he took me with him in his service to Göttingen and treated me in a very friendly way. But as he wanted to travel from there to Paris via Frankfurt I refused to accompany him further since I had an implacable resentment against France and the French. For that reason I left him, went back to Hamelin, was given a pass and journeyed to Lemgo where I worked for a year with a Sauerland master. I had scarcely been fourteen days in Lemgo when the French advanced into the town and my master got six men for billeting. These guests were already hateful enough to me in themselves but they became even more so since they behaved in such an arrogant and domineering manner. The food was not good enough for them and each evening they wanted schnapps and beer. One of them demanded yet another pleasure and wanted to compel my master to go with him. When I saw my master's fright I offered my company and led the Frenchman behind the wall where there were deep dung pits. However, it was too much for the Frenchman; he took hold of me and wanted to thrash me, but I extricated myself from him, ran against him and pushed him into a deep dung pit.

Then I returned to my master, told him of my adventure with the Frenchman and cleared out, since he had not come back. I spent the night with a friend of the leatherworker's miller. This friend had already served with the English-German Legion, had deserted in the expedition to north Germany and now had no more ardent wish than to dare to go back to his corps, but fear of the fighting held him back. He persistently advised me to go with the English-German Legion and described service with it so pleasantly that I made the firm resolve to follow his advice. However, it was hard to get to England because of the French and my master in Lemgo would not let me go so I remained with him for about a year.

Then I travelled back to Hamelin with the firm resolution to go to England as soon as possible. The few weeks that I spent in my birthplace were a prelude to my impending future. One day I went with other fellow tradesmen to the Berkelschen look-out, a place for dancing half an hour from the town at the foot of the fortress that was in the possession of the French. After we had begun to dance some Frenchmen appeared from the fortress. They first interrupted our dance, then, as various people had come up to them, demanded with drawn swords that we leave the place. We yielded, withdrew and considered whether we should let such behaviour go or whether we were a match for our troublemakers. After a short deliberation we made for the fence, pulled the stakes out, manned the house and courtyard doors and the bravest of us went into the hall. Scarcely had the first got in than the Frenchmen immediately attacked us with their swords, the strokes fell on both sides, the floor was discoloured with blood, our people moved forward. The Frenchmen drew themselves back into a corner and already a majority of them lay stupefied on the ground, then they spoke favourably and asked for protection. We came to an agreement with them, laid our stakes on one side and had a drink with them so that the battlefield was suddenly changed into a happy party.

Meanwhile we got the news that one of the French in the heat of the battle, unnoticed by us, had jumped out of the window and was already rushing back with help from the fort. So much did the French redouble their friendliness and seek to detain us that we deemed it advisable to make off, escaping through the nearest door while they, so we were told, were already posted. We circled the town, over Klein Berkel, the Ohrberg, Ohr and Tündern, where we crossed the Weser and, after we had carefully washed away the blood, we arrived separately at the Osterthor. It was high time we did so, since the hurrying French reinforcements followed us still, if in vain, up to the foot of the Ohrberg.

On another Sunday evening I went with some of my friends onto the dancefloor; we waited quite modestly in front of the gate. But the French would not tolerate this; they abused us as *'paisans',** which was very displeasing to us; we retorted 'cur'. Then they pressed forcibly upon us and brought us to the door of the house with cudgels. Some French pursued us onto the street where it was dark; here some telling punches were traded and on the next morning the corpse of a Frenchman was found there. I experienced such events frequently and so little could I bring myself to do it, lest I make a mistake, nevertheless they put me off staying longer in my native town and reawoke the longing for England in me again.

---

* 'peasants'.

With one of my young friends, the garden boy Kruse, whose father had been a Hanoverian soldier, and who shared with me the hatred of the French and the desire for adventure, I had often consulted how we could most easily achieve our disappearance since our parents refused permission for our departure. At last we set a day and Kruse ran away at the break of day. But his mother, who immediately missed him, came to our house to make enquiries; I was held back by force while the father hurried after his son and immediately caught up with him. The young man refused to return, all remonstrances did not help; the father used force, but the son threw himself on the ground; the father thrashed him, but in vain. At last the father threatened to hurry to the next village and to get the police to pursue him. That worked and the young man calmly went back home. Now we were kept a careful eye on, our clothes were locked up and we were never left alone so that it was impossible for us to fix a fresh escape. But that could not persuade me to give up my resolve.

THE JOURNEY TO ENGLAND

As Lindau has already recorded, he had been advised to join the King's German Legion (KGL) by one of its deserters. Britain had traditionally relied heavily on foreign corps because of her limited manpower and the need to maintain her global commitments. The quality of these corps varied widely during the Napoleonic wars, but that of the KGL was second to none.

Following the disbandment of the Hanoverian army in July 1803, many officers and men had made their way to England, where they were formed into the KGL. Further recruits swelled the Legion's strength after Napoleon withdrew nearly all his troops from Hanover in order to attack the Austro-Russians in 1805. This enabled a British expeditionary force under Lord Cathcart to land in the Weser estuary and occupy Hanover at the end of the year, before being withdrawn in February 1806. In August 1805, the strength of the KGL had been just under 6,900 men of all ranks, but by May 1806 it had doubled to over 13,300. This was little short of its peak strength, reached in 1812, of over 15,000.[1]

The KGL was an integral part of the British army. It contained ten battalions, including two of light infantry, five cavalry regiments, artillery batteries and engineers. But maintaining these units at full strength proved problematic: it was now more difficult to draw recruits from Hanover, as Lindau's own experiences showed. Thus, the original Hanoverian recruits became diluted by a range of nationalities, including Poles, Illyrians, and men from various German states, and by volunteers from among prisoners-of-war in British hands. Desertion was common, but the professionalism of the officers, most of whom were Hanoverian, preserved the KGL's high combat value.

Lindau's voyage to England took him past the island of Heligoland, thirty-five miles off the German coast. Captured from Denmark in 1807, it served the British as a base from which to recruit men from Hanover and smuggle goods into the European continent in defiance of Napoleon's trade embargo. The island would remain in British hands until 1890.

Lindau mentions seeing some of Schill's men on his way to England. In April 1809, following the outbreak of another war between Napoleon and Austria, a Prussian officer, Major Ferdinand von Schill, led his regiment, the 2nd Brandenburg Hussars, out of Berlin to try and liberate Prussia from French domination. After failing to spark an uprising, he rode north in the hope of reaching the sea: he himself was killed at Stralsund on 31 May, but some of his hussars escaped.

Lindau records that, when he ran away from home to go to England, he was followed by his younger brother, Christian. Although Lindau forced him to return, Christian did later enlist in the KGL as an artilleryman.

It was on St Martin's Day of the year 1809, a Monday morning, that I left my parental home. I took nothing with me, except the clothes that I wore, my trade, half a gulden, a shirt, which I had hidden the Sunday before, and besides these a stick. I hurried unnoticed to outside the Osterthor; only my little brother, who had heard that I wanted to go to England, ran after me and asked me persistently to go back to Mother, who would grieve very much. But when he saw that his effort was fruitless he demanded that I should take him too. As much as my haste allowed, I urged him to go back; one hour from Hanover on the hill of Rohrsen, when I saw that no one was following, I earnestly asked him to go back again and drove him back with blows. That was the parting from my family.

Towards evening I was in Hanover and the next morning I hurried towards Bremen. Three hours beyond

Hanover I met a painter's boy who was well known to me; he told me that his trade was now going badly and immediately seized on the resolution to go with me, when I had made my intention known to him. Since my companion was furnished with money and provisions, but I was stripped of everything, he supported me as far as Bremen, where I argued with him in the painter's business since I did not want to go to the shoemaker's inn for fear that I might be persuaded to get work. The painter went out to pick up his money, and I went on the streets to look for some ten-penny pieces. When I had some groats in my pocket I noticed a policeman and he pursued me; but I was soon out of sight and luckily I reached the painter's shop again.*

Meanwhile my fellow traveller had already carefully laid the table and asked me to take a place. But, however great my hunger, I was not willing to taste the food since I reckoned that our cash would hardly suffice; but my companion, who noticed my anxiety, laughed at me and said I should let him worry about that: the meal would not cost us a penny, he was already practised in that. After the meal we left the inn with the promise of paying if we came back, and the innkeeper let us out without ill will since the painter left his knapsack, which indeed stood on the torn oilcloth and was stuffed with hay. I stood meanwhile in great anxiety, constantly afraid that someone would chase after us and I kept looking back; however we luckily came into the Oldenburgische. My companion changed his mind here and went into

---

* Begging without a licence was illegal.

Oldenburg; I turned back to the Weser to look for a way of escaping to England.

Since my reserve of money was very small I had to claim men's pity and never in these days did I lack black bread and buttermilk; nor did I go without in the evenings – when I reached an inn I ate hot potatoes, slept on straw and paid one gutengroschen the next morning. During these days I met a peasant who told me, to my great joy, about the Englishmen, who often landed to throw off the customs and smuggle in goods. I remained with this peasant for a day, made him a pair of shoes, thereby earning myself a groat, and hurried on. Another time, before I crossed the Weser, I saw myself forced to take four days' work in order to earn the necessary money for board on the rest of the journey. At last I reached Ritzebüttel, where a man in red uniform immediately lighted upon me; although he could not understand my language, I made it plain to him that I wanted to go to England to become a soldier.

He brought me to a house on the water in which I found a marine with a gun at the ready together with seven men in blue uniform with red facings and round hats open at the side. They were, as they later told me, people from Schill's Corps, who had escaped from their chief and sought refuge on an English ship in order to be able to continue to fight further against their hated enemy of their native land. After half an hour an officer came from a warship lying near; he questioned us in broken German, and promised us that we would soon be collected, and then shipped away again in his little boat. A bigger boat soon took the eight of us to the ship, where we were taken to the second deck. It was dark here; we were so hungry and felt so lonely and abandoned that we were first weak then fearful that we might have been deceived. Then a sailor brought us a dish of salt meat and ship's biscuit; we relished the food and took heart again. After some hours we felt a burning thirst and the sailor took us to a barrel up on the deck; we scooped water out with a metal cup, but it was foul and only great thirst could get it down.

When we were on the second deck again we felt very wretched. My thoughts about my parents distressed me; I wanted to write a letter to them, and one of Schill's men declared himself ready to do this. I looked for an officer and asked him for permission to write home. He asked me where I came from; I named Hamelin on the Weser where the fortress had been destroyed. He seemed to know it; he gave me paper and a pen. Kipp, one of Schill's men, gave me ink, another called Normann wrote the letter for me.[*] Both were making a start in the cavalry of the legion but I never heard anything more of them after that. When the letter was ready I handed it over to the officer, who took care of it, but many must have wandered from his care as I discovered in Harwich, where one of my brothers[†] – who was a butcher – met me, and who came to England with the same intention as me.

On the same day, about six o'clock in the evening a boat came to our ship. There was a cry from above: 'Germans come up'; we did not understand it until a sailor made a sign. When we arrived on top, we saw a large boat lying to; we took leave of the officer, who encouraged us by saying

---

[*] Lindau was obviously illiterate, though he later at least learnt to sign his name.

[†] Georg Lindau.

that we would soon be in England. Then we boarded a boat that the sailors all battened down and left us alone under the deck where it was very dirty from the coal for which the ship was used as a transport.

Then a wind got up and we could only hold on with an effort. We soon lay on one side, soon the other, soon we sailed with our head in the deep. I thought I would be lost, thought of home, of my parents and regretted the step I had taken. Schill's men themselves lost courage, which these people had never lacked otherwise; it was certainly no longer solid German soil beneath us, even if there was still German heaven above us. The storm raged throughout the whole night; we often heard the sailors cry out loudly and we believed our ship would go under, then we heard them speaking normally again, which raised our courage. This terrible situation, in the dark hold of a ship made more filthy through our sickness, did not improve. We cursed our decision: we would never have gone on the ship if we had known beforehand; now and then we were afraid that we had been deceived. At last the ship was still; we were glad, but our happiness rose when through the opened hatch light again fell into the darkened hold. Someone made a sign to us. I was the only one who could stand; the others crawled up the steps supported by me. The sailors helped us but appeared to be used to such a scene and laughed at us if we complained of our distress to them.

Quite near, perhaps a half an hour away, lay the island of Heligoland, a rocky crag; up above people worked windlasses, with which they hoisted goods from the ships. High up on the rock, which was reflected in the water, stood a lighthouse on which various flags would be hoisted. In circles around us we caught sight of floating barrels that, we later discovered, marked the dangerous places; seagulls flew round in thousands, they settled thickly on the ship and appeared to be pleased, as we were. After a while an open boat suddenly drew up near our ship, which was designated to take us off. With our dirty things we climbed up from there, soiled from head to foot. We had of course washed ourselves, but without success since the filth on our hands and faces only became worse, and rubbing with the sailcloth only made it more immovable. We soon reached the bigger ship lying nearby and a small ladder was arranged for us to climb up. Here we immediately had to wash ourselves with fresh water and soap, which had great results, whereupon a doctor examined our state of health and declared it satisfactory.

On this ship things went better for us; we were shown a corner on the upper deck to which we brought our things, we then examined the ship and were glad at its fineness and cleanliness. Soon a sailor came and brought a wooden bowl with salt meat, ham and ship's biscuit and in a friendly way invited us to eat. We ate a little biscuit, but we did not like it; the sailor saw it, went off and soon came back with a white jar of peppermint tea, a bag full of brown sugar and two little bowls of rough china. We drank the tea; the sailor was pleased that we were happy and looking about in a lively way, and he invited us again to eat some meat, which we refused since it was repugnant to us. Now we enjoyed the remarkable view on the right and entertained ourselves by watching the many ships sailing by. We saw many a white point appear in the distance, come nearer and evolve into a fine majestic ship that sailed past us. The sailors frequently came near us, looked at us politely and praised our resolution to become soldiers, but laughed when we said anything.

In the afternoon the ship came under sail; the anchor was wound up on a long cable that the sailors pulled, which we helped with. Some of the sailors went up the mast and stood on the yards; we were horrified and were continually afraid one might fall in the water. The ship quickly cut through the waves and everything on it was in regular motion. A sailor had a big piece of lead, like a clock weight, with which he measured the depth of the water and at the same time investigated the seabed and the bottom by means of a piece of wax attached to the lead. Another on the stern with a clock and a book stood in contact with him and measured the speed of the ship. Close in front of the steersman stood the compass, which looked like the face of a clock. Then the sun sank into the sea like a great fiery wagon wheel, the starry sky arched above us all and around us; there nothing but water, in which the stars glittered, so that we appeared to be floating in a boundless sea of light.

In my heart were mixed pleasure, fear and hope for the future. In England, I thought we would go against the enemy at once. We turned down the food that we had asked for this evening. At about ten o'clock we had to leave the deck; we lay in our corner on the level and I pushed my bundle under my head, but the motion of the ship prevented me from lying like that so that I positioned myself, like the rest of them, against the side of the ship, but did not sleep and only wished to be on land. The time passed very slowly. The monotonous slap of the waves increased the tedious quiet. Only every two hours the sailors struck a big oar on the deck and woke the relief; each time it gave us a shock and we were frightened that the ship might have struck a rock. At last the light of the morning broke on the shiny cannonshot on the deck into our darkness and brought solace and hope to our despairing souls. We hurried on to the deck and saw the fiery ball of the sun lighting up and filling the sea with shining splendour.

In Camp at Bexhill

Lindau reached the port of Harwich in East Anglia on 27 July 1809. He claims that he stayed there at the depot for some weeks, but his memory was mistaken. He was actually transferred within days to Lymington in Hampshire, and on 17 August reached the KGL's general infantry depot at Bexhill on the Sussex coast.

The KGL's arrival in Bexhill five years earlier had already had a major impact, for the town had only around a thousand inhabitants. At first, the troops had to live in tents, but soon built huts. One of the officers, Major Christian von Ompteda of the 1st Line Battalion, recorded in August 1804 that the inhabitants looked on the KGL troops 'much as we do on Cossacks', but later described how the gentry had visited the camp, and how 'they seem to be beginning to discover that we are not quite outlandish bears'.[2] Relations warmed with time, and the parish registers soon began recording marriages between KGL men and local women.

In 1989, local enthusiasts set up the Bexhill Hanoverian Study Group to uncover their town's KGL connection. A permanent exhibition can now be seen at Bexhill's museum, and a commemorative sign was unveiled by Lady Elizabeth Longford at the former cemetery where over 150 KGL soldiers and relatives are known to have been buried.

Lindau joined the 2nd Light Battalion, and was placed in the 1st Company. His uniform was broadly similar to that of the British 95th Regiment of Foot, the famous riflemen to whom the novelist Bernard Cornwell assigned his fictional hero, Richard Sharpe. Lindau's battalion wore dark-green jackets with black collars and cuffs, black leather belts, black stovepipe shakos, and grey trousers. It was distinguished from the 1st Light Battalion by jackets with three rows of buttons on the front, rather than just one; by a pompom on the shako, in place of a plume; and by black tufts, instead of rolls, on the shoulders.

Initially, one-sixth of the men in the KGL light battalions were armed with Baker rifles, which were accurate up to three hundred yards, over three times as far as the smoothbore musket carried by most infantrymen. The rifle could be used to fire about one aimed shot a minute, but in an emergency, the balls could be loaded without their greased patches, reducing accuracy but quickening the rate of fire. The proportion of rifle-armed men in the KGL light battalions was later increased to one man in three, and eventually all the men carried them. The battalions were formed with just six companies, but were gradually expanded to reach a full complement of ten by May 1812.[3]

It was rare for the whole of a light infantry battalion to be deployed as skirmishers. Most of the unit tended to fight in close-order formations, for skirmishers alone could not check a powerful attack as they were unable to fire a concentrated volley or make a united charge. Yet light battalions were commonly used to cover an advance or retreat, or to hold villages or farms in front of the main position, and Lindau's battalion would repeatedly fulfil such roles.

The first commander of the 2nd Light Battalion was Lieutenant-Colonel Colin Halkett. He came from a distinguished military family and had initially served in the Dutch army, following the example of several ancestors, before helping to raise the KGL. Towards the end of 1811, while serving under Wellington in the Peninsula, he took command of a brigade composed of both the KGL light battalions, and by January 1815 he had been knighted and promoted to major-general. His younger brother, Hugh, also served in the 2nd Light Battalion, and commanded it during the 1812 campaign in the Peninsula before being transferred to the 7th Line Battalion.

When Lindau first reached Bexhill, the bulk of his unit was absent, for the two light battalions had joined an expedition in July 1809 to destroy the French ships, arsenals and dockyards in the Scheldt estuary. The expeditionary force of 40,000 men took the outlying island of Walcheren and the fortified town of Flushing, but failed to attain the most important objective, the great naval base of Antwerp. Furthermore, the troops were stricken by the deadly effects of Walcheren Fever, which appears to have been a combination of diseases including malaria, typhus and dysentery.[4] By the end of December, the KGL light battalions had returned to England, but nearly half their number were sick, and many men were debilitated for years by the after-effects.

On the other side we noticed land; it was the object of our desires, 'England', we were told. At about seven o'clock someone gave us bread and meat, we did not want to eat it but put it in our bundles. Soon we entered the harbour through a crowd of ships, among which there were many large warships, and we lay close to the land, where four men from a German depot were already waiting for us. Having climbed up on land we could not walk: we lifted our feet high up and were like drunken men. Our compatriots – among whom there was a Sergeant Meyer who had been posted in Hamelin and who asked me about this person and that – received us in a friendly way and led us to the barracks, which lay a quarter of an hour from the harbour. Here we found recruits from Germany who had already arrived earlier, whom I did not know. They shared their food with us, we gave away our meat. The first thing that was handed to us was a blue knapsack, which we took good care of.

Soon after midday there came an officer from the Light Troops, who asked which branch of the service we wanted to serve in. Schill's men chose the cavalry, I the green rifleman's uniform that Sergeant Meyer, who himself wore it, had very much commended. We stayed at this depot in Harwich for some weeks; we received our rations daily: a pound of bread, vegetables at midday and meat and four pence (equal to three silver groschen). If I bought myself in the morning one pennyworth of bread, cheese for a halfpenny and one pennyworth of beer, I still had a penny halfpenny, with which I usually bought extra bread since otherwise I would not be full. At the end of each month we got in addition five to seven shillings so that in the course of time I had saved up two pounds six shillings, with which I bought myself a silver watch.

There were many new things that we got to see here, which alleviated the tedium; the clogs of the women and their red cloaks attracted my attention. Underneath the clogs in the middle of the sole they had a round piece of iron that was fastened with two- or three-inch-high supports that left tracks in the sand like those of a donkey. The working people and peasants had two-inch-thick soles, on which it was very difficult to walk, but the people walked very slowly and deliberately. A pleasant way of passing the time for us was to look for flints, which we shattered and kept beautifully marbled pieces; we also caught crabs on the shore when it was an ebb tide, cooked them in the barracks and ate them with much pleasure. Almost every day we looked for grey winkles, cooked them and drew the creatures out with a pin; they tasted very good to us. In the inns, where beer was drunk, cooked winkles like this also stood on the table, one could eat them as one pleased. One sight that we saw in these days increased our longing to be sent to a regiment soon: there were, I dare say, seventy or eighty ships full of soldiers who with fife and drums went past at Harwich one morning – a heart-stirring sight.

In the middle of the winter, in a light frost, at last we seventeen men marched with Sergeant Meyer and two soldiers from the barracks to the headquarters at Bexhill. On our march we passed the great city of London with its fine houses and many people on the streets; without making a halt there our march through it lasted some hours. Later, Schill's men left us; I had always kept up a good friendship with them, although as cavalry they were always somewhat stuck up. The sergeant also turned back again with his men. Some people from the headquarters had welcomed us and with them we reached Bexhill after some more days' march.

Here we were immediately given our clothing: we got shirts, shoes and a uniform and we were allowed to sell our old clothes. Drilling began: three hours in the morning and two in the afternoon; for the rest of the day we had to polish and clean the barrack rooms. After fourteen days I did my first watch, which pleased me greatly. Several weeks flew by until the expedition came back from Flushing. Almost all the troops had had the fever and the greater part of them had been buried in Zeeland. From one battalion that had been a thousand men strong scarcely four hundred came back, and they felt so ill that they could scarcely drill and ended up in the hospital again and again; however, they would gladly carry out their duties. Thus it took longer, perhaps a year, for the regiments to be made up to strength again.

In the second year of my stay in this place I was made the servant to Lieutenant Denecke, who commanded our company, so I reluctantly parted from my weapon. There in England each soldier is obliged to be a servant for four weeks at the request of an officer; if he refuses to do this he is kept under arrest for the same period of time, so I was forced to do this. After the time had passed I asked again and again for my dismissal, but in vain, even though I did not go to any great trouble to please my officer since this service was not to my liking. I got particularly angry over the uniforms, which the officers had got their servants to make and which looked so odd that I refused to put them on. I was only persuaded to put myself in a clown's jacket,* in spite of the mockery of my comrades, after a serious threat from my officer.

One day it particularly annoyed me that I had to wait at table; for that reason I went angrily into the cellar and drank a glass of beer. Soon afterwards I had to carry plates out of the hall; I stumbled into the anteroom and dropped some eight beautiful new plates to the ground, plates decorated with the name of the battalion. From fear of punishment I made myself scarce; I ran first into the kitchen then into the cellar where the beer was poured out. Meanwhile my officer, who unfortunately might well have got a report of this, pursued me and forced me to wait in the hall. Now I excused myself, saying I was indisposed: I could no longer provide table service since I had drunk beer in the cellar. My officer sent me home on this account, but came out right after me because he felt unsteady himself. In the fresh air we were both drunk and fell down the high steps that were in front of the house. In his anger at this he accused me of throwing him down; but I denied responsibility and he brought me into the guardhouse at once.

Here my friends made fun of me, that such a boot black as I should come into the guard house in a dazzling jacket, and made me so angry about it that I took off my clown's jacket, flung it into the open fire, lay on the wooden bed and slept until the next morning, when my officer came

---

* As a mess waiter.

back and took me out of the guardhouse. Although I asked urgently to be allowed to stand under arms again, since I had been admitted as a soldier, not as a servant, I had to perform the hated service for longer still and could not reach my goal yet. I played another trick by which I hoped to get my freedom. My officer sometimes let two harpists come from a neighbouring place. Late one evening I had to escort one of them back home; we came to a defile and I took the lady on my back but fell down where the mud was thickest, with her underneath and brought her home thus badly treated. The next evening my officer appeared again and berated me, but I was not successful, since I would not be set free from my hated service until we had been in Portugal for three months.

2

THE PENINSULAR WAR
1811

The KGL never fought as a complete, independent corps. Instead, it was a pool of battalions, cavalry regiments and batteries, some of which were detached to a particular theatre and combined with British or foreign units to form larger bodies.

In the summer of 1809, for example, at the time that Lindau reached England, four of the line battalions were stationed in Sicily, while the other four were serving in the Iberian Peninsula, along with the 1st Hussars. The two dragoon regiments and the 3rd Hussars were in England, while the 2nd Hussars and the two light battalions had just sailed on the ill-fated expedition to Walcheren.

It was not until 1811 that the two light battalions left England once more, this time to join Wellington's army in Portugal, and with them went Lindau. The Peninsular War was already in its fourth year. It had begun when Napoleon tried to seize control of Portugal and Spain in order to enforce his trade war with Britain and secure the south-western flank of his empire. When the French occupation provoked widespread revolts, Britain sent an expeditionary force, and Napoleon had to intervene with massive reinforcements in November 1808.

After recapturing Madrid and reversing the situation, Napoleon himself returned to France in January 1809, but left behind over 280,000 men to complete the subjugation of the Peninsula. In the autumn of 1810, a French army under Marshal André Massena invaded Portugal. Wellington had to withdraw to Lisbon, but held on to the city behind the specially constructed Lines of Torres Vedras during the winter. Then, on 5 March 1811, Massena began to retreat, partly because his troops were starving, but also because he had learned that Wellington was about to be reinforced by sea.

These reinforcements included the KGL light battalions, which landed at Lisbon on 21 March. It was not the first time they had served in the Peninsula: more than two years earlier, before the Walcheren expedition, they had taken part in the Coruña campaign, and had been evacuated by sea in January 1809 from the north-western coast of Spain.[5] But Lindau had enlisted after Coruña, and so for him personally, 1811 brought his first experience of active service.

Lisbon had suffered a devastating earthquake in 1755, and Lindau records how the inhabitants feared a repetition. They regarded Wellington's troops as Protestant heretics, even though many of the soldiers were actually Irish Catholics and few were genuinely religious. Later in his account, Lindau scornfully describes some of his off-duty brawls with Portuguese soldiers. But such friction hides the fact that Portugal was indispensable to the British as a base for driving the French out of the Peninsula. Wellington depended on Portuguese manpower and resources: he had reformed and rebuilt the Portuguese army, and incorporated its units into his British divisions.

As much as one-third of his field army in the Peninsula was Portuguese.

The Voyage to Lisbon

At last, in the New Year of 1811, we were embarked at Portsmouth; about twenty men at a time were taken in a boat, conveyed to the big ship and boarded it by means of the rope ladder that hung down. I was among the last since I had to accompany my officer while he first bought coffee, tea, rum and sugar. Then I too boarded the ship with the greatest hope and rejoiced that the boring life in England was at an end. Nevertheless I have never since had it so good as during my stay of about one and a half years in that fortunate country. After we had lain at anchor for half a week we sailed off, to the loud rejoicing of the troops. For some days we passed between England and France, and left the coast of England out of sight. At last the chalk cliffs of Land's End faded away as we steered for the open sea.*

During this time our troops were for the most part already seasick; it went no better for the officers and since the servants also succumbed, I had to wait on my officer, which was very difficult but I always kept cheerful. If it was at all possible, I hurried to my comrades in the lower hold with tea, which I always kept ready to revive them, since they lay with pallid faces and distraught looks in the filth, which they were constantly adding to, and

---

* Land's End is actually granite.

wanted to die. I kept myself better since I could always draw breath in fresh air, except at night, when I rolled up in my blanket and slept under the stairs; I often had to go on deck to get fresh water. One evening I was sitting with some of my comrades on the benches by the rudder when suddenly a great fish at least forty feet long rose up, blew a out a mass of water and opened its mouth so wide that we started back in fright lest it devour us. The sailors laughed at us and said that this fish would bring us a storm.

By the next day the sea began to become restless; soon the waves grew higher, the ship rolled a great deal and the sailors took down all the sails apart from the most forward and highest on the foremast. The storm lasted five days and five nights, during which we were in constant fear, which reached its height when in the night we suddenly heard a terrible crash. The sailors let out a cry, the officers fell out of their berths, I too hurried up to the deck. We could not see anything amiss there, but the storm raged so dreadfully that we could not remain there, so we hurried down again. We soon realised that in the confusion of the storm another ship had run on to our bowsprit and that it had broken. When the storm passed, the troops had to clean themselves and their surroundings and then there were some calm days on which we killed time by catching blenny and gulls, which tasted very good roasted.

Some days later there arose a disturbance in the night: there was a fire in the captain's cabin. A servant had not put out the light and the table had caught fire; we poured fresh water on the fire and smothered it completely with wet blankets. In the fine weather I settled myself in the crow's nest for hours on end. From there I could see the distant land, it might be the coast of Spain or Portugal; I gladly stayed up there since on the deck we were very often disturbed by the sailors. One day a rock was pointed out to us in the far distance with the observation that it was Gibraltar – the storm had driven us so far to the south. Near Portugal a Portuguese pilot came on board, an amusing fellow who greatly entertained our officers with his lively dancing. In Lisbon harbour a crowd of boats appeared with oranges and fresh loaves; for a shilling I got a surfeit of oranges, which refreshed me; I did not want to eat the bread, which was made from maize.

When we were disembarked the next day the troops of the line came into the barracks; both our light battalions got quarters in the city. Now we could recover from the hardships of the voyage; we got ample rations, did not need to drill, looked at beautiful Lisbon and spent the time cracking bitter almonds that we ourselves picked off the trees. One evening a warship gave us a magnificent spectacle: it caught fire in the harbour and, in spite of every effort to save it, the whole thing was consumed by the flames. Our agreeable rest was only soured in this way by a prophecy that Lisbon would again be convulsed by an earthquake, which was universally believed, and by the fact that we had to be on guard from the inhabitants, who took us for heretics – many men who walked about on their own had already been killed or robbed of their clothes.

Badajoz

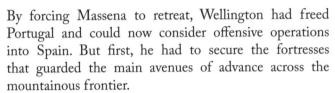

By forcing Massena to retreat, Wellington had freed Portugal and could now consider offensive operations into Spain. But first, he had to secure the fortresses that guarded the main avenues of advance across the mountainous frontier.

In the south, a French force under Marshal Jean-de-Dieu Soult had captured the powerful stronghold of Badajoz, on the Spanish side of the border, on 11 March 1811. Wellington therefore detached 18,000 men under Marshal William Carr Beresford to counter Soult and safeguard the eastern approaches to Lisbon.

The KGL light battalions formed an independent brigade, one that had not yet been attached to a division, and it was pushed forward from Lisbon to the Portuguese frontier fortress of Elvas as part of Beresford's wing.

Wellington decided personally to reconnoitre Badajoz before trying to capture it, and so he temporarily left his main force in the north and joined Beresford. Wellington was escorted during this reconnaissance on 22 April by the KGL light brigade and two Portuguese squadrons. But while he was examining the walls of Badajoz, a company of the 2nd Light Battalion was badly mauled when caught between a sortie from the fortress and, from the other direction, a French working party on its way back from the woods where it had been sent to cut timber. Lindau records his relief at escaping from this dangerous situation. After the sortie, Wellington completed his reconnaissance right round Badajoz, and that evening Lindau's brigade returned to Olivenza, fifteen miles to the south-west, having been under arms for seventeen hours.[6]

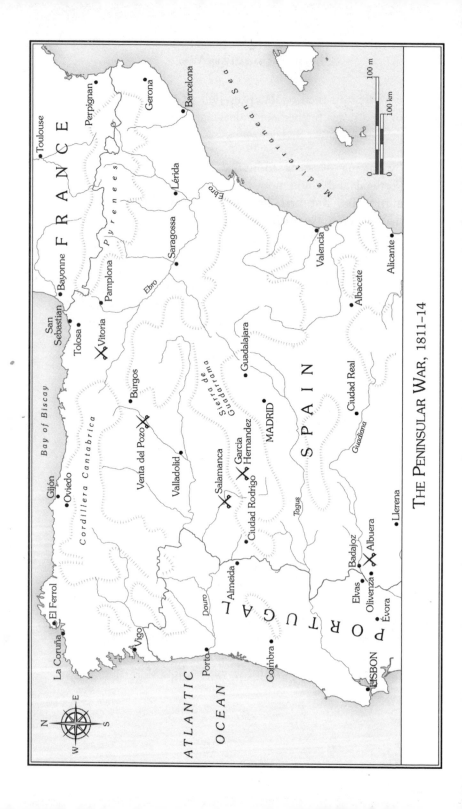

THE PENINSULAR WAR, 1811–14

Wellington then rejoined the bulk of his army over a hundred miles further north, leaving Beresford to begin operations against Badajoz.

One morning I heard our bugler blow the signal for departure and immediately our brigade, both light battalions of the King's German Legion, was assembled; we marched out, made only the usual days' marches and in some weeks reached Badajoz. The day before we had come into a place, Olivenza, where the people, as was usually the case, had hidden all their valuables and provisions. But a soldier in the field, even if he gets supplied with his daily pound of bread and meat according to the commissary's weight, has a persistent overwhelming hunger; he looks for provisions, knows where to find them and sits himself down in spite of strict prohibition, in spite of all the provosts with cords and lashes in their possession. With one of my comrades who had learnt pharmacy I looked for provisions in a loft and found in a corner a packet with flies on, which I angrily threw away and observed that the people here must get very bored. But my comrade took the packet and kept it, then went with me into the local chemist, sold the packet with the flies and paid me four Spanish thaler; he kept an equal sum himself. We continued our investigation and in a wooden shed I found three casks of bacon; I set a piece in front of me and gave the rest to my comrade as a reward. Then we got the order to march again, so we packed up our things together with

the bacon, drank a flask of wine with the fly money, heard
the signal for departure, were assembled at the appointed
place and marched towards Badajoz.

At about eight o'clock in the morning we made a halt
for an hour, and heard the news that a significant number
of Frenchmen with a cannon had been marched into a
nearby wood, but they were marching further on, so we
could not detect the enemy there and we reached a hillock
half an hour from Badajoz, from where we could look over
the whole town. We were dispersed as skirmishers, and
had to lie down and pay attention to what was happening
in the town. Soon we noticed that the French, since the
gate was already barricaded, were coming out of the town
one by one round a door post and then, when a column
had assembled, they tried to avoid being spotted by going
into the roadside ditch. When there were enough of them
they marched round the hill and attacked us in the rear
out of a wood; we marched back over the hill, where the
enemy set large dogs on us, which bit the legs of some
of our people. Nevertheless we crowded into the wood
under steady fire; there I found my brother the butcher,
whom I had been very anxious for during the fighting.
But he had known how to look after himself very well and
had grasped one of the attacking dogs with an arm round
its head and clasped it tightly with the other, alternately
giving it a thorough thrashing and coaxing it so that the
dog, which he now held on a lead, soon became docile
and got used to him.

We embraced here in heart-felt happiness over our
deliverance since the French had already withdrawn and
some of our people had died. 'Now we want to live once

more in an ordinary way, dear brother; I have a piece of bacon,' I said to him.

'And I have something to drink,' he replied.

Our captain and another officer, who also felt hungry, shared our meal so that we had nothing left. After the companies had been inspected it was found that we had lost some fifty men; then at around five o'clock in the evening we moved out of the wood and marched back to Olivenza, where we reached our former quarters very late.

Our host received us with a grumble and reproached us that his bacon had been stolen, as far as I could understand Portuguese, about which I had a guilty conscience. When I got up from my straw bed the next morning I went to my captain to clean his clothes; I complained to him that the peasant was so angry and spoke all the time about a stolen pig. He might well mean the bacon that I had taken out of the cask and on which we had eaten heartily yesterday after the skirmish. My captain advised me to appease the peasant and if he could not be pacified to bring him to him. With this comfort I went home and asked my peasant why he was so angry; he showed me the empty cask and again began to chide. I said to him that yesterday he had had Spanish and Portuguese quartered with him. If he meant that we were the thieves he should accuse us in front of our officer. The man's wife took up my offer and went with me to our captain, who listened quietly for some time, but when the woman began scolding him that the German riflemen were robbers my captain took hold of his sabre hanging on the wall, at which the woman rushed out of the room. My hosts were quiet now, we remained with them for a few days yet, but avoided seeking bacon or ham, and then marched back again in the direction of Badajoz.

About an hour from this town both our battalions halted and camped. Here we repeatedly heard the cries of the storming line battalions that lay in front of the fortress; we expected that the ranks would also approach us. At noon one day we departed, believing that we were going against Badajoz, but we marched past the town in the direction of Elvas. On this route we reached the Guadiana; we waded through it, and the water came up to our arms, but we were not permitted to drink it although we were nearly dying of thirst. Then there began a gradual ascent, where the heat was so intense that two men suffocated.

In the afternoon the sky covered over, it became as dark as night; we saw the lightning and heard the thunder roll, but it did not rain yet. We arrived at a wood, quickly undid our blankets and laid three or four on top of one another, with us underneath. Big raindrops fell, like pigeons' eggs, and soon the rain came down in streams and such a thunderstorm began that we thought the trees would fall down together on top of us and the wood stand in flames of light. After half an hour the storm receded, it was light again and we crept wet through from under our blankets. Corporal Weissleder, who had lain under a blanket with me, complained that someone had played a dirty trick on him during the storm and had cut off the buttons of his gaiters. I looked at his gaiters and found that five buttons were melted off. A bolt of lightning, which had killed a sentinel, must indeed have struck close by. When we had stayed here for some days we departed in the direction of Elvas. We camped about an hour from the fortress in a wood where we found the line troops of the English German Legion, which was a great joy to me since among them I found compatriots whom I had not seen for a long time.

Elvas

Whereas Lindau had only recently arrived in the Peninsula with the KGL light brigade, four of the line battalions had been deployed there since 1808. As he records, some of his old friends were serving in their ranks.

Elvas was the Portuguese twin of Badajoz: these two fortresses lay ten miles apart, and guarded the passage across the frontier. By the end of 7 May, Beresford had invested Badajoz. Lindau's brigade was among those used for this operation, but was not seriously engaged, unlike some British and Portuguese units, which lost a total of 733 men while constructing trenches and batteries under fire, or repelling a sortie by the French garrison.[7] (Lindau is mistaken when he recalls the British actually attempting to storm the fortress at this stage.)

Early one morning, after we had taken leave, I went into Elvas with one of these friends, Heinrich Reichert from Hamelin, a musician from the 2nd Line Battalion who beat the big drum. At the side of the town, on a high hill I saw the low wall of the castle that was called the 'key to Portugal'; around the hill lay great iron drums fastened with an iron chain that could destroy a rushing enemy trying to storm the castle. The town itself is embellished with fine towers and with many bulwarks round it. We walked in through the narrow gateway, bought some salt, which a soldier in the field particularly needs, as well as tobacco and rusk. The bread in the bakery looked as fine as gingerbread and was very cheap. We bought one and immediately started to eat it, but the bread baked from maize tasted so coarse and like sawdust that we threw it away. The baker laughed at us, got hold of the bread again and took it back into the house. In the market we bought fine oranges that refreshed us very much and of which we each put ten in our haversacks.

Then we had one drink in an inn and set off for home, but on the way we met some Englishmen from the garrison who almost forcibly marched us back to the inn, where we had to sing German songs to them, which the Englishmen very much liked to hear since they could only sing badly and on their own or not at all. While singing there was some heavy drinking until we did not want any more wine (to which they added sugar) and they obliged us to drink and sing continuously. When we realised that we had already drunk over the limit we at last departed, in spite of the attempts of the Englishmen to hold us back with the most friendly words and who seemed very happy to stand us drinks and to listen to the singing. In the hall in front of the shop stood some Portuguese soldiers, with whom my comrade immediately got into a quarrel. I walked in and wanted to drag him out of the crowd since the whole hall was full of Portuguese. But when one of them grasped my bayonet from behind, I got hold of it, drew it and immediately hit out at the Portuguese, at first with the flat of the blade and blindly. My comrade followed my example and we both tried to gain the door of the house with the blunt edges. Although the Portuguese drew their bayonets on us our blows fell so thick and strong that they all, some fifteen men, fled into a large room where they barricaded themselves in with benches and chairs in order to be safe from our pursuit.

We made our retreat to the street, where some twenty Portuguese awaited us with bayonets. We urged each other on and attacked sharply – the Portuguese fell back, we gained the open street and met four Englishmen who immediately stood by us, since the English and the Germans always held together against the Spanish and the Portuguese. Now no one followed us any further. We hurried to the gate but found it was already closed. As we wondered how to get out and I tried the depth of the moat by dropping a stone, we heard a carriage trundle along behind us. We pressed hard on the gate and when the NCO opened it we got into the open with the horse.

We lightheartedly breathed open air again, ran back to our camp and informed the corporal, but we were already too late: we were at once reported and were put under arrest. We passed our time with the fire guard by telling our comrades of our adventure in Elvas, since anxiety about the inquiry from the citadel kept us awake. Next morning I was led before the captain; I tried to excuse my lateness, but did not tell of my adventure and received the verdict that I would get no leave. After some days, during which my worries about an inquiry constantly gnawed at me, we marched back before Badajoz, where we lay for some weeks more, almost inactive since we were not needed to storm. Only now and then did we have to stand to under arms at night while the English stormed the citadel, though always in vain. The next day we often saw piles of dead bodies that the English themselves had left lying at various places under the wall.

BATTLE OF ALBUERA

Within days, Beresford had to lift the siege of Badajoz when Marshal Soult marched 24,000 troops from southern Spain to relieve it. Wellington had given Beresford permission to fight a battle to prevent Soult reaching the fortress, so long as the odds justified it. Beresford was joined by Spanish forces under Generals Joachim Blake and Francisco Castaños, and a bloody battle ensued on 16 May at Albuera, thirteen miles south-east of Badajoz.

The KGL light brigade held the village of Albuera itself as an advanced post, but the heaviest fighting raged further south, where Soult drove into Beresford's right wing. At a critical moment, Beresford ordered the KGL light brigade to abandon Albuera, in order to have a reserve in hand should it be required. Four Portuguese battalions were deployed to cover the evacuation, but according to Lindau they mistook the KGL for French troops in a case of friendly fire. The KGL then received a cancellation of the order to pull out of Albuera. Only a few French infantry had so far occupied the village, and they were swept out by the KGL.

By the end of the day, Soult had been checked. But the heavy casualties called Beresford's handling of the battle into question, and his order for the KGL to evacuate

Albuera village was later misinterpreted as a sign that he had lost his nerve and was preparing to retreat.

The KGL light brigade's losses were relatively light. Lindau's battalion lost just 7 per cent of its strength, whereas six British battalions had losses of more than 60 per cent. One of those units, the 1st Battalion of the 3rd (or the East Kent) Regiment of Foot, or 'The Buffs', lost a staggering 85 per cent of its men.[8]

Lindau's account of some men of his battalion eating horsemeat after the battle is confirmed by his company commander, Ole Lindam, who described how:

> We young fellows soon found out that we were ravenously hungry and so, while some gathered splinters of gun carriages and the like, others made rough gridirons out of broken ramrods which were lying all about the place and others cut steaks out of the bodies of the horses that had been killed, and grilled them over the fire, and I don't think I have ever had a better dinner in my life.[9]

Lindau himself was less enthusiastic.

One morning we received the order for departure; both our light battalions marched off at about midday and came by ten o'clock in the evening to a large heath near Albuera. We lay down with our packs full, with our rifles to hand; towards morning we heard a great deal of noise and when it was daylight we saw we were on the left flank of a great army of English, Spanish and Portuguese.

Near the village that lay in front of us stood a twenty-five-foot-high tower where we had an outpost. I sneaked into the village to look for provisions and noticed my brother standing on guard up on the tower; he asked me to bring him some wine. In a house in the village I found an old man who did not want to leave and who lamented that his wife had taken all the provisions with her. Other houses were quite empty; only in a stall did I find a sheep, which I took with me. When I again came near the tower my brother called to me that I should kill the sheep quickly, hurry back to my company and warn them that the enemy was advancing. I at once slit the throat of the sheep and let it lie by the tower so that my brother might remove it. I warned our commander of the proximity of the enemy and hurried back to the tower with the adjutant. From high up the tower he saw the enemy, but he came back down quickly with my brother and ordered us to hurry to our companies and not to take the sheep with us since the enemy was already here. Nevertheless I cut off a leg and hurried back; but scarcely had I tied it in my pack than our company advanced against the skirmishers.

We pushed forwards through the village and occupied a field opposite it with eight- or nine-foot-high thistles,* through which we moved quite unnoticed as far as a little river. On the other side of the river were enemy skirmishers who fired on us persistently; behind them were troops of the line and cavalry. We also fired continuously; for all that the enemy pressed over the river many times, we drove them back from it again with fixed bayonets. Soon we heard strong fire from the whole line on our right and saw that the battle was in progress. We might have been

---

* Probably marsh thistles, which can grow to over six feet in height.

fighting for about one and a half hours, in which we lost many people, though the enemy even more, when we had to draw back because the Portuguese stationed behind us were to take our places. Here we came under fire from two sides, since the Portuguese took us for French and shot at us until our Colonel Halkett chased the Portuguese away and threatened the commander himself with a sabre; at this time a bullet tore away my piece of mutton, which I had bound to my pack some hours before, and another pierced my canteen.

We now marched through the ranks of the Portuguese and stationed ourselves behind the village, where we immediately received the command to take up our earlier position again since the Portuguese had yielded to the French. We placed the bayonets on our rifles and with a 'Hurrah!' went into the village, which was already occupied by the French. They began to shoot at us, but fell back with such haste that on my own I chased some ten Frenchmen out of the ruins of a house and could only reach the last with my bayonet, which, as he jumped over a wall, I ran through his body. The French fell back over the river, we again took up our former position and the fighting continued until evening, during which the French constantly led fresh columns against us but none of them was in a position to dislodge us. However, the thistle field was in the end so shot to pieces that that it was no longer able to protect us. Towards evening the enemy, who were Alsatian and spoke German, called over to us that it had been plenty enough for the day, they wanted to cease fire; we might do the same. So it became quiet on our flank apart from the rain that had not ceased all day and still constantly poured down in streams, and from the centre to the right of us we could hear all the time heavy fire and a cry of 'Hurrah!'

When we saw the watch fires of the French half an hour away we marched back to the camping place of the previous night. I had to stay as an outpost on a piece of ground to the left of the village; I found a soft place to lie down but the cold and the storm as well as a disgusting stench in my nostrils did not let me sleep the whole night. So I stole very stealthily into the village to look for food. Here I suddenly heard a low moan; I went towards it and recognised an officer of our battalion, Captain Heise, who, with his face covered in blood, asked me in a faint voice to shoot him to death. I shuddered at such misery and comforted the man – of whom I was fond, for he was a true friend to the soldiers – with kindly words, that he should be patient, it would soon be better for him. Then I lay some hay under his head, hurried back to my outpost and lay down again. Next morning I realised that my soft camping place was a body that had been covered over with a little earth, and of which the feet still stuck out.

After we were detached from the outpost at noon we paid a visit to the battlefield. A mass of wounded from our side and the enemy lay there, infantry and cavalry, private soldiers and officers, among a multitude of dead. The day was very hot, the unfortunate men called out for a drink of water, which we fetched for them from the neighbouring stream and eased the agonies of the death throes since we could not comply with the wish of most of them to be shot. Close by a wall was Captain Heise with a bullet through his head, already dead.* I was heartily thankful that I had been fortunate enough to come through, since death had been really close to me too four times; apart from the shots already mentioned I had got a bullet through my shako and another through my coat tail.

Towards evening I left the battlefield; the cries were weaker, most of the wounded were already silent, and these two freezing nights might well have freed them from their dreadful agonies. We slept in the camp under the open sky, while cold and hunger tormented us because by this time nothing had been supplied for two days. The Poles in our battalion had already cut pieces of meat for themselves from the dead horses and eaten it raw, loathsome fare to the rest of us; I was always too disgusted to eat it, although I enjoyed my food. At last, towards the end of the next day came the long-awaited refreshment after we had spent three days quite without food and drink, working in the heat part of the time.

The next morning we crossed the river and arrived at the encampment abandoned by the French, but found nothing in the wood except a crowd of wounded and dead Frenchmen. We lit a fire but had no food, so I went with a comrade further into the wood to take young birds from their nests; we did not find any but were richly compensated in another way. At a clearing in the wood two donkeys were grazing, one old and one young. At once we chased after the animals and succeeded in chasing the young donkey fast into a thicket; we were not allowed to shoot it. We slaughtered it at once, took the meat and

---

* Captain Georg Heise in fact died at Elvas on 10 June.

turned back to the camp, where our arrival brought about great rejoicing; we roasted the meat and in no time it was eaten, since many good friends turned up to enjoy the excellent donkey meat.

After we had pursued the enemy for some eight days we marched back the same way again and arrived near the battlefield of Albuera. After two hours on the road an indescribably horrible stench came over us. The dead had been burnt and made the air so contaminated that we could not eat. In addition the water from the river was undrinkable on account of the nauseating smell it had received from the bodies that lay in it. So we broke camp again after a few days, marched in every direction, often until the dead of night. We were on our feet again before dawn and would cheerfully have put up with all the exertions if we had not had to fight hunger all the time, since our rations were so small that we often consumed in one day what was supplied to us for three. We tried to help ourselves as best we could: we fried congealed ox blood with some olive oil that the peasants gave us, willingly or not, and roasted the bellies of the oxen slaughtered for our battalion, a dish over which we often fought bloodily.

3

THE SALAMANCA CAMPAIGN
1812

After Albuera, Lindau's brigade was incorporated into the 7th Division. This was the last and most junior of Wellington's infantry divisions, having only been created on 5 March 1811. It had a high proportion of light troops: of its three brigades, the British and KGL brigades were composed wholly of light infantry, while the Portuguese brigade included a battalion of *caçadores*. It was also largely foreign: even the British brigade contained a regiment of Chasseurs Britanniques, composed of foreigners in British service. Not surprisingly, the division was popularly known as 'the mongrels' because of its mixed composition. It lacked the renown enjoyed by some of the other divisions, for it never had as colourful a commander as Major-General Robert Craufurd or Lieutenant-General Sir Thomas Picton of the Light and 3rd Divisions; nor was it given much chance to distinguish itself until the fighting in the Pyrenees in 1813.

Throughout the second half of 1811, Wellington had faced a stalemate. But then Napoleon withdrew troops from the Peninsula to strengthen his planned invasion of Russia, and he also ordered the conquest of Valencia in eastern Spain. Both these moves weakened the forces directly opposed to Wellington and enabled him to take the offensive into Spain in 1812.

First, he took two frontier fortresses: Ciudad Rodrigo in the north on 19 January, and then Badajoz in the south on 6 April. Lindau did not take part in either siege. His division was part of a detached force, under Lieutenant-General Sir Thomas Graham, which helped to cover the siege of Badajoz in case Soult tried to relieve it from the south.

During this time, Graham made several expeditions to try and surprise an outlying division of Soult's army under General Jean-Baptiste Drouet, Count d'Erlon. This was the reason for the night marches that Lindau describes. He begins with a vivid account of the bid to intercept 1,800 French troops at Llerena, seventy miles south-east of Badajoz, in the early hours of 26 March. The advance ran into a French cavalry picket, which charged Graham and his staff, chased them back on to the 7th Division, and threw his column into disorder. Having lost all hope of surprise, Graham reached Llerena to find that the French were already abandoning it. His troops were too tired to launch an effective pursuit.

The Expedition to Llerena

One evening as it became dark we received the order to strike camp; we marched the whole night in the greatest quiet. Towards morning, when it was still quite dark, the generals, who were close in front of us, came and mixed with us. I marched on the left flank and jumped to one side with the man behind me as we heard the trotting of a horse close to us and could hardly see anything. The horse pressed through the gap, where it reared up and knocked the corporal marching behind us to the ground, where he died instantly. In the same moment some shots fell on us and twenty-four men of our company, including me, were ordered beside the cannon – of which there were two on our right side and two on our left. The twelve of us were posted some eight yards in front and to the side of the two cannon on our left; we at once received the order to lie down and now the cannon thundered over us from behind, while we were covered with a shower of fire. Then we went forwards; we advanced through a little wood in which we found some rifles, a saddle and some sabres by an extinguished watch fire, the remains of a cavalry outpost some twenty men strong.

As we walked out of the wood, we saw, as day began to dawn, a large nunnery, from the windows of which white towels were waving and friendly greetings called out. We marched past it, heard cannon fire to the right and left of us and advanced towards a near-lying town behind the nunnery, from which the cannon fire greeted us. Then we got the order for our battalion to drive the enemy out and marched left around the town while an English regiment marched round the town to the right. We ran so suddenly that several of our people remained lying down; we could not catch the French, who moved out of the other side of the town in a mass towards the mountains, instead we turned back with the English after we spent some hours in vain pursuit.

We marched into the town and each received two rations of wine and one of bread, which refreshed us very much. Towards midday we again advanced outside the town and marched past the nunnery, where our officers had been invited to stay by the nuns, who stood inquisitively in front of the nunnery. Meanwhile, merry from the rations we had received, we started to sing cheerful songs and the band played lively marches, and so we came at nightfall to the earlier campsite again and took up our old places. The next day the provisions that we had captured in the town were distributed – Clerena* was the name of the place – but soon hunger gnawed at us again. We did indeed once try cooking a vegetable that grew in abundance in that neighbourhood, but became ill and so we remained with our niggardly rations.

Later, when we had marched several days' journey farther, in the evening we saw a large herd of sheep. Roll call had already been sounded and everyone had lain down to rest, but desire for sheep drove me on, together with five of my comrades. Well armed, so that we would be up to a provost guard if any came across us on the way, we slunk out of the camp. Our guards, who well knew what we intended, at a favourable moment did not see us, and after we had travelled a good hour in the darkness, we scented the herd near, to our delight. Immediately the dog barked, we heard the shepherd come nearer with a big Alsatian that he had on a cord; I spoke to him and ordered him to hold the dog back. He asked what we wanted; I replied, 'Nothing but some sheep.' He called another shepherd,

---

* Llerena.

who also brought with him a large Alsatian. I thanked my comrades' foresight; we cocked our rifles and told the shepherd that we would shoot them dead together with their dogs if they released them.

When one of the shepherds began to be abusive we encircled them and one of my comrades stabbed one of the dogs with his bayonet through its neck and impaled it to the ground. Now the peasants pleaded for their lives and that of their second dog; they would give us what we asked for. One of the peasants had to look out four fat beasts for us and tie them up. We offered money for them, but the shepherds did not want it, so we departed with our booty. On the way back we slaughtered the sheep, removed their heads, cut them in pieces and returned to the camp in an excellent mood with full knapsacks. But the guards received us with the news that there were peasants in the camp and that a search would be held. We quickly hid away our meat in the ground, hastened to dry our shoes, which were wet from wading the streams and which could give away the fact that we had been out of the camp, but we had scarcely lain down than we had to fall in. No one was missing, the sheep were not found anywhere, so the peasants were chased away with a reprimand.

At this time night marches were especially burdensome. Once we marched on a pitch-black night from evening till dawn and travelled only one and a half hours' march because we moved first forwards and then backwards and often halted for half an hour. Since I had not slept the previous night and since many of my comrades fell in deep ditches and hurt themselves, and others had bruised their faces on the rifle butts of the men in front,

I walked out unnoticed at midnight close by our whole column and lay down to sleep again by the side of the foremost ranks of our 1st Battalion, which was in front. I must have slept for some hours; it was still night when I was wakened by the frost, but my battalion had not reached me. I marched back to it again; my absence had not been noticed.

Some days later we were skirmishing with the enemy from ten o'clock in the morning until evening and pushed them back victoriously. When we had halted in a village, I went out with one of my comrades and not long after, we began to head home with our bread sacks full of potatoes. Close to the village we met Commander Halkett, who asked what we had been doing.

'We have fetched some water,' was our answer.

'Does one fetch water in a bread sack?' he replied, and ordered us to open them. When he saw the potatoes he ordered us to follow him, although we assured him we had bought them with our money. Near the village I whispered to my comrade that this could be a bad bargain and when we came close by a hedge, I said, 'I am going to do a bunk.' 'So am I,' he said. We chased along the hedge through some of the village gardens into our quarters.

Decamp was sounded on the spot; we quickly moved out with our weapons; the battalion had to form up and Colonel Halkett scrutinised all ranks to find the escapees again. My heart beat faster when he came near me, but I had pulled my shako down over my face and assumed an outlandish expression, which a freshly painted moustache usefully assisted. He did not find the miscreants but gave a general reprimand, spoke with the officers and NCOs and charged them with discovering the potato thieves. The following days we went rather short since we did not dare start on the booty that we had only obtained with such a fright. When this storm had blown over we allowed ourselves to enjoy the potatoes in the evening, and they were not turned down by the NCOs, who doubtless noticed that these were the potatoes for which they were meant to be looking.

At that time my brother was ill and went into the field hospital. I asked my sergeant for permission to spend the night with him. By the evening he was so ill that the doctors gave up on him; I was very troubled by that, but able to get some wine from the cellar that lay under our feet, on the advice of a sick Pole. Under the straw on which my brother lay was a loose floorboard that could be pushed to one side. I climbed into the cellar where there were very big barrels and drew out many buckets full – so many that my whole company drank plenty on the next day. I gave my brother as much as he could drink of the strong wine; he complained greatly of thirst and I took him for lost. It made him hot and red in the face but the next morning he was better. I did this for two nights and got a great deal of wine for my comrades; then to my great regret we moved on again.

'*COCHONS HANOVRIENS!*'

Some days later it happened that I, Sergeant Schmidt and ten men were quartered in a house in front of which was a deep ditch with a narrow footbridge. In the evening, when it had already become dark I went out of the house and over the bridge; suddenly I heard behind me loud abuse and saw that a peasant had grabbed my sergeant from behind and wanted to push him into the ditch. Then I seized the peasant by the throat and pushed him hard against the wall and took him into the house with the help of the sergeant. Here we asked the peasant why he had taken hold of the sergeant and we beat him so long that he admitted that he had wanted to kill the sergeant in order to take the pewter buttons on his uniform, which he took for silver. The peasant was immediately brought into the guard, he had to march with us for some days and after he had been severely whipped by the company he was given his freedom again.

Another time we were camping near a peasant, whom we asked for some wine, since we knew that he had a whole cellar full. Since he would not give us any, on my advice we paid to have wine fetched for us, drank to the peasant and made him drunk. Next I demanded again that he give us wine and when he still refused we gave him a beating in which everyone helped so that he could not say that any one of us had done it. Then the peasant went out of the house to accuse us before the commander, but we went with him and brought him to Adjutant Riefkugel, to whom we preferred to turn on such occasions. Here the peasant accused us of mistreating him, but we brought up the fact that he had drunk wine with us so long as we had it and his whole appearance showed that he had drunk more than a little. When he refused in due course to set out his wine, he had had some from us, so now we merely asked for as much wine back from him as he had drunk of ours that we had bought while he had his whole cellar lying full. Then the adjutant reprimanded the peasant to comply with our reasonable claim and drove him out. When we came to the house the peasant, who now appeared undeceived, brought us ample wine and we drank boldly.

Gradually the peasant got into such a condition that he did not really know what was going on around him any more; then we took some hens away from him, cooked them quickly in other quarters and ate them in our house, where the peasant himself tasted them without suspecting that he was consuming his own hens. On the following morning the peasant was so friendly that he sold us wine, at first for money, but then on account, since we told him we received our pay before we marched off. Each of us made two tallies, of which the peasant kept one, on these we carefully cut notches; our man was glad that the number of notches increased more and more on his sticks, and we had plenty to drink and thus good days. But when departure was sounded some time later we had no money and our tallies had vanished. The peasant with his tallies ran after us as far as the assembly place and stood at a respectful distance, and then turned to Lieutenant-Colonel Halkett, showed him his tallies and complained about his trouble in which we repeatedly heard the word '*Krab, krab*'. The officer showed no desire to be inconvenienced and said to the peasant, 'Nonsense "*krab, krab*", clear off away from the front!' The peasant slunk off looking distressed with his expensive sticks in his hand; after this he would never again lend to a soldier on a tally.

Soon after this we had to move into winter quarters in some villages, where we remained for several months and as often as we could we went to the mountains to get goats that we chased about wildly and found very difficult to catch. Since we were not allowed to shoot them we forced the creature into a narrow place, took out its legs with cudgels and carried it home. Apart from this we had to be satisfied with what we had; it was a poor district and we had nothing but our daily rations. When the rainy weather came to an end we struck camp and encountered the enemy almost every day, but seldom came under fire despite frequently hearing violent firing in the distance. The French skirmishers did not like to have dealings with us: we met at a great distance and the French bullets often struck the ground in front of us because the enemy's rifles were bad, and their powder was very coarse; besides which we understood the trick of loading and shooting lying down. Our adversaries knew us well enough, when they abused us as '*voleurs*' and '*cochons Hanovriens*'* if we were near enough to them; we abused them less, shouted over 'cur' and singed their hide.

At this time, when our food was very scarce, numbers of our people deserted to the French, which was very easy to do since in a few yards one could be with the enemy. To prevent this, we often had to stand to secret posts at night, in which a good half died because the groups of deserters, always five to ten men strong, overcame these posts. From our battalion ten buglers deserted and only a few Poles. One of these was captured again and, since there was no

---

* 'Cheats', 'filthy Hanoverians'.

opportunity to shoot him, he was hanged. The provost guards to whom this execution was committed hesitated to do it and gave a bribe of five thalers to one of our sappers by the name of Stuckenschmidt, who had already served under all the rulers. This man stood the Pole on a cart, strung him up with a rope to the branch of a tree and withdrew the cart from under him. Through this deed he drew the hatred and contempt of the whole battalion on himself; little time was wasted, as one might say, before he was murdered by one of our people.

When one day I, with six other men, was ordered to the baggage, we came by a chapel. I went in to look round for food, found absolutely nothing, but was alerted by a knocking that came from a deep cellar. I went in carefully with drawn bayonet and found a horse, which, tormented by millions of flies, was constantly stamping its hooves on the ground. I led the horse out of the cellar and the chapel and freed it from the flies and I had just handed it over to a soldier's wife who was by the baggage, when suddenly some twenty wild pigs appeared, as it seemed to me, falling on us out of a wood nearby. I shot one dead; scarcely had I fired the shot than an English staff officer burst out on me and called me to account for it. My justification was in vain, he drove me away, and soon came back with a hussar who brought me to the provost guard one and a half hours away. I was there until nearly evening; the provost officer came and asked why I was there, I shrugged my shoulders; he asked the commanding NCO, who replied that no report had been handed in, so the provost officer said that I should get away, my battalion lay over there. I hurried out, heard the cannon already thundering in the distance, came to my battalion, reported to my sergeant and told him of my adventure. He reassured me that if I went straight back under fire, no more would be asked about it.

After a concluding skirmish we advanced at nightfall into a pine forest, where we had scarcely lain down when I heard a cry nearby. It was one of our buglers, bitten in the face by a scorpion. The doctor came to him, cut a big piece of flesh out of the man's cheek and took him to the sick bay, from where he soon came back healed. Since that time we regularly, before we lay down, searched the place thoroughly for scorpions. They are especially to be found in the bark of fir trees, and we cut them up with a bayonet. As a protection against these creatures, in Spain there is a large number of fine lizards, some one foot long, gleaming green with white patches, which will always run over the face of a sleeping man when a scorpion is near and wake him up. This happened to one of our people, by the name of Ohms, who got up angry at the unending nuisance of the lizard, but when he wanted to put on his shoe and emptied it out a scorpion fell out. These lizards were so beautiful and became so tame that for our amusement several of us carried these creatures all the time in our bosoms or in our rucksacks.

On one of the following nights we were camped in a village; suddenly the alarm was sounded because the wolves had broken into our herd of oxen. Our forty men marched out; already in the distance we could hear a horrible howling; we shot into the air and the wolves fell back. When we got to the herd of oxen we shot rapidly at the hunting beasts and drove them back into the rocks.

BATTLE OF SALAMANCA

A brief lull followed the fall of Badajoz. Then, at the end of May, Graham was summoned northwards to join Wellington for an offensive into Spain from Ciudad Rodrigo. The advance began on 13 June and reached the city of Salamanca four days later. Wellington besieged the city's forts, three convent buildings that had been converted into strongholds. Lindau vividly recalled these forts, for his brigade was ordered to try and suppress the fire of the defenders while a position was constructed for a battery. But it was not until 27 June that the forts finally capitulated, the delay being caused partly by a failure in the ammunition supply for the besieging guns.

Wellington's immediate opponent was Marshal Auguste Marmont, the commander of the French Army of Portugal. During the siege of the Salamanca forts, Marmont had actually appeared north-east of the city, but had not dared to attack Wellington's strong covering position. He fell back northwards behind the Douro river, but was reinforced to a strength of 50,000 men, about the same numbers as Wellington had under his control. On 16 July, he therefore took the offensive, with the aim of outmanoeuvring Wellington and forcing him to retreat back to Portugal by threatening his lines of communication.

By the morning of 22 July, Marmont was eight miles south-east of Salamanca, and was beginning to circle clockwise round the city. Wellington, who was on the inside of this turning movement, was resigned to ordering a retreat, for he would not risk a battle without a clear-cut advantage and knew that Marmont was about to receive further reinforcements. But in his eagerness to pursue, Marmont made the mistake of allowing his army to become over-extended. Wellington seized the opportunity for a devastating counter-attack, starting in the west and then progressing eastwards as more divisions joined the assault.

The 7th Division, which had been involved in some minor skirmishing on the eastern flank in the morning, was transferred to support one of the attacking formations, the 5th Division. But the KGL light brigade saw little actual fighting: Lindau's unit, the 2nd Light Battalion, lost just sixteen officers and men killed or wounded, or 3 per cent of its strength.[10]

Lindau mentions standing during the battle near some Brunswick troops, another of the British army's foreign units. In 1807, Napoleon had absorbed the Duchy of Brunswick into the German satellite state, the Kingdom of Westphalia. The dispossessed duke had to take refuge in the Austrian Empire, where he raised a corps to seek revenge, and uniformed it in black, with death's head badges. When war broke out between Napoleon and Austria in 1809, the Duke of Brunswick tried to start an insurrection in central Europe, and then fought his way more than 250 miles to the North Sea coast, where he was evacuated by British ships. His men were formed into a regiment of hussars and one of light infantry (known as the Brunswick-Oels Jägers). In the Peninsula, most of the infantry was assigned to the 7th Division, and brigaded with the KGL light battalions.

Not long after we moved up in front of a castle near Salamanca. Here the Englishmen had already set up batteries with which they succeeded in silencing the cannon of the fortress. I remained for the day near the wall of a cloister that lay at the foot of the castle and I had to help cook for the company. At night we slept in the cloister while all around us there was continual cannon and small-arms fire. Next morning I had to lie in the upper storey of the cloister, where a multitude of firing holes had been made, through which we always kept our eyes on the fortress and the gunners who came forward to the shutter, so that only seldom could a cannon be shot off; and our battery fired merrily against the fortress. In the afternoon at four o'clock a big barracks higher up collapsed; there was a terrible crash of stones and beams mixed with the screams of the people. Only the back wall of the building remained standing, on which we saw every rank of uniform hanging. From the ruins a thick smoke arose that the French tried to extinguish, but they came directly into our line of fire and many died, while only a few of our men were hit.

My sergeant, by the name of Lüder, had the misfortune to be mortally wounded here. He demanded that I fire rapidly although the order given was that we should only shoot if an artilleryman came forward to the shutter; he grabbed my rifle from my hand, laid it down and before he could shoot was hit by a bullet in the cheek. After three days he was dead. We were relieved from this post by Portuguese troops who surrounded the citadel more closely and then, as I heard later, forced its surrender. After our withdrawal we had continual fighting until we came to the neighbourhood of Salamanca.

On the day before the battle that took its name from this city it was fine weather but the air was sultry and our marching was very difficult. At about four o' clock in the afternoon the sky suddenly grew dark; we received the order to put our rifles together and to lie down covered by our blankets some twenty yards away. But before we had lain down the rain was already streaming down, accompanied by dreadful lightning and fearful thunder. This storm lasted only about an hour but the thunderclaps crashed so close above our heads and the air was so full of fire that we thought our last day had come and we were struck with fear and horror. At other times I did not have the time or inclination to pray, but in this tumult of the heavens I prayed to God that he might graciously let the tempest pass us by. When the sky had again become clear and the sun was shining warmly on us we checked our weapons, extracted our bullets and loaded them again; then we wrung out our blankets to dry them, since otherwise they weighed down the pack too much. We had no provisions, so we cooked chocolate – which we had bought in a town the previous day – in water, cut up ship's biscuit in it and enjoyed it. Then we lay down and rested for the whole night.

When the sun rose – it was a fine, light morning – we got up, packed our sacks, made ourselves a warm drink in our service kettles from what was left over from the day before and marched forwards for half an hour to the edge of a wood where our cavalry had halted. In front of us at the fringes of the same wood stood French cavalry and infantry. Our cavalry immediately attacked and chased the enemy riders back but had to retreat before the fire of the French infantry; whereupon we advanced, firing against them but were pressed back and then our cavalry made a successful attack, so that the enemy marched sidewards towards our right flank. We too now marched to the right and reached a part of the battlefield where the Portuguese had already stood under fire. A great crowd of wounded men lay here, mostly with their legs shot off, crying out piteously, especially if we touched them, which was altogether unavoidable since we had to march in columns. We saw an enemy battery draw up opposite us, and in an instant it decapitated seven men from our eight companies, including Lieutenant Finck; immediately we looked back but Adjutant Riefkugel commanded, 'Forwards, men! Nothing has happened.' Now we were drawn up in line, on the right* next to us the Brunswick men, I had the left flank; suddenly a cannon ball completely took away the man on the right flank of the Brunswickers near me altogether. The man behind lay there with his body open, he stood up, pushed his bowels into his belly with his hands, fell down and died.

After about half an hour we marched left towards the enemy and stormed a hill that was occupied by French infantry who kept up a strong fire on us. We dispersed as skirmishers and fired continuously; our cavalrymen too helped us to force back the enemy, at which the battery that had caused us so much damage drew back. After we had followed the enemy for about a further half an hour it was evening; we marched back a little, lay down in open country and went to sleep with our rifles to hand, hungry, but very tired.

---

* Properly 'on the left'.

Garcia Hernandez

The two KGL dragoon regiments were in the cavalry spearhead that Wellington sent to pursue the French army after Salamanca. On 23 July, the cavalry came upon the French rearguard, a division under General Maximilien, Baron Foy, at Garcia Hernandez, nine miles east of the battlefield.

What followed was one of the most outstanding cavalry charges of the Peninsular War, for the KGL dragoons managed, without support from other arms, to break intact infantry battalions. Normally, horses would instinctively shy away from the hedge of bayonets of infantry formed in a square, and the cavalry's best chance of breaking into the formation lay in intimidating the men into panicking and breaking ranks. It was all the more impressive an achievement as it was the first time that the KGL dragoon regiments had carried out a charge – since arriving in the Peninsula six months earlier they had seen only skirmishing.

Lindau gives the impression that he actually witnessed the action, rather than simply passing over the field afterwards. Yet even Wellington's leading infantry (the 1st and Light Divisions) arrived in view only when the action ended.[11]

Next morning, after a ration had been circulated and we had taken position near our dragoons in rank and file, we were inspected by Wellington, after which our cavalry pressed forward in pursuit of the enemy over a narrow bridge.

We followed them but had to halt in front of the bridge because they checked our march, and here a heart-rending sight met us. At the access to the bridge lay a French infantryman with his back leaning against the riverbank; his eyes, nose and jaw had been cut off, so that each time he breathed two streams of blood flowed out over his neck. Compassionately, and shocked by the sight, several of us went to him to bring him help; I too held him in my arms, while he pointed with his hands towards his heart, he could not speak, he wanted to indicate that I should stab him and my officer too urged me on. Though I gladly would run my bayonet into the body of an enemy, I had with deep sadness to leave this unfortunate man to his fate.

After we had crossed the bridge and had traversed a very difficult passage on the other side we came to a pasture where we found two of our dragoons just cutting down a grenadier square; between them lay many of our cavalrymen with their horses. We hurried at the double in the same direction towards the high ground in front of us where a third square was just being attacked by our dragoons. The foremost horse fell on a bayonet, in a moment three or four other cavalrymen jumped over the fallen horse into the square and struck out at all around them. The troops became disordered, the cavalry prevailed on all sides and in a few minutes the whole battalion was struck down; those who threw their weapons away and ran were brought in by the cavalrymen and taken prisoner. We marched over this field of bodies and I have seen the legend with my own eyes – one man had been cut in two – such was the power with which our dragoons swung their very long handsbreadth swords. Afterwards the fourth square ran away from our cavalrymen, but almost all of them were taken prisoner. The French cavalry, which had halted behind them, turned tail and we reached the top of the hill without having to fire a shot. We followed the enemy almost until evening. Now and then a regiment would sit down, but as soon as our fearsome dragoons sprang forward they took to their heels. When it became dark we pitched our camp near a village where our dragoons lay, so that they could rest after the exertions of the day, as was their due, while a Portuguese cavalry regiment with two cannon was pushed further forward still.

So far as I could, fully armed, I stole into a chapel that lay not far from us near the village, since I had been told that the French had had a bread store there. By the light of the perpetual lamp that still burned I searched, discovered oats and breadcrumbs scattered on the ground but I could not find anything for myself. While I was searching every corner I suddenly heard a cry and shooting in the village, and then the trumpets sounded. I assumed it was a surprise attack by the French, went to the door of the chapel and listened as crowds of cavalrymen dashed out close by. I took them to be French and went back and hid myself in a big hollow statue of Mary that stood on the altar. When I heard a German detachment outside I left the chapel and went to our camp, but found it empty. Very soon after, I came up with our 1st Battalion and stationed myself on the flank, then

Portuguese cavalry hurried past us; they were pursued by the French, on whom we fired, and soon after they were chased back again by our dragoons.

My neighbour, whom I asked about my battalion, directed me to the right around the village. As I ran in that direction I met the company farrier of the dragoons, I believed he was called Becker and came from Latfede near Hamelin; in response to my question he showed me the place where my battalion was stationed and added that I need not hurry: it had just come back from the pursuit of the French: 'That must encourage us, but I have not flattened them good and proper on their noses.' I reached my battalion in low ground and marched forwards with them into a wood the same night, where we stayed until morning. For the next days we were stationed close to the cavalry, which frequently rode to attack the fleeing enemy, and after some time we came into the region of Madrid.

The Liberation of Madrid

Wellington's army entered Madrid to a rapturous welcome on 12 August. The city had been under French occupation for nearly four years. Napoleon's brother, King Joseph of Spain, had already abandoned his capital, but had left behind a garrison of 2,500 troops to hold its citadel, a network of fortifications at the Retiro. As Lindau describes, these men were forced to surrender.

Even in the distance this city was very impressive, with its many towers and great palaces. We advanced without finding any resistance into the most beautiful city I have seen in my life. Our whole battalion was quartered in a large building that resembled a barracks* and we rejoiced that after many weeks we could now sleep with greater comfort, even if it was on a stone floor. The following morning my comrades hurried into a church that had served the French as a magazine and where they found shoes and articles of clothing; I came too late, found it thoroughly cleaned out and satisfied myself with a steelyard that I found under some hay; I immediately offered it for sale in a neighbouring merchant's shop and was relieved of it for ten thaler. When I went from there into the market I saw a crowd of poor people lying on the ground, appealing to the passers by, but receiving little charity. These poor tattered people ate gooseberry skins that lay on the ground around them and assuaged their hunger. I too knew the pain that hunger brings; out of pity I bought a great mass of gooseberries, since I had a large sum of money in my pocket, and shared them out. These unfortunate people, wasted away to skeletons, kissed my hands and thanked me with deep melancholy but almost knocked me over in the eagerness with which they strove for the gooseberries.

To avoid this scene of misery I left them but could not help hurrying to the market each morning that we were in Madrid and refreshing these people with my rations, as also did many of my comrades. Very often, though,

---

* It was a deserted convent.

we found some who had succumbed in the night from hunger and cold. Then we bought fresh bread, which tasted better than ship's biscuit. After some days the French surrendered the citadel, I saw them coming out in rank and file. They confidently handed themselves over to the English but were later transported to the coast by the Portuguese and there it must have gone badly for them since, when we later marched on the same roads, we found numerous bodies of these poor Frenchmen, robbed of their clothing; this made us angry at the despicable conduct of the Portuguese.

4

Retreat from Burgos
1812

Wellington left Madrid on 31 August. He drove the French Army of Portugal, which he had defeated a month earlier at Salamanca, north-eastwards along the main road leading to France. But his advance was checked when he reached Burgos. Although he occupied the city, he tried in vain to capture the castle on the hill above the city.

In Wellington's hands, the castle could have blocked the main French line of communications, and hence made their entire position in the Peninsula untenable. But the threat had provoked them to take drastic measures. In order to concentrate overwhelming numbers against him, they withdrew their forces in southern Spain.

Wellington had no choice but to retreat. On the night of 21–22 October, after a dispiriting, thirty-five day siege in which he had lost over two thousand men, he began his withdrawal. The 7th Division was the last infantry division, and was covered by a cavalry rearguard. Lindau vividly describes the precautions taken to ensure silence, lest the troops came under artillery fire from the castle as they crossed the bridge in Burgos.

The Siege of Burgos

From Madrid we marched north, the French constantly fell back before us, without us having to shoot, but in the mountains near us we heard copious cannon fire. In short days' marches we moved forwards and after some weeks had passed we moved to a camp on a hill about four hours' march behind Burgos, where we remained for over eight days. Beneath us in a village lay the dragoons, another mountain extended to the right of us, occupied by the French, with their outposts stationed in a village at its foot. Although we had strict orders not to leave the camp, a night of hunger drove us to a sheepfold that lay in front of the village occupied by the French.

Our commander's interpreter, Wassinger, who was also cook at the mess, led the party, which was composed of eight men; we took two mules and a quantity of rope and passed our outpost, whom we instructed appropriately. On arrival at the sheepfold we opened the hatch as gently as possible, I climbed through it into the fold, unbolted the door from inside and bound the sheeps' legs, with the help of two of our people. Meanwhile Wassinger and the five others protected the way out of the village but immediately came back and informed us that a French cavalry patrol was approaching. We gently closed the door, stood closely pressed together with our two mules at the side wall of the sheepfold and awaited the enemy, ready to shoot. But when the cavalrymen turned round at the end of the village we again occupied the way out, loaded up our mules very quickly with about ten sheep and hurried back into our camp where the outpost let us through without challenge, as previously arranged. When an inquiry was held the next day, because a complaint had been received, we buried the meat and Wassinger marked the still-living sheep with the mess marker and so nothing suspicious was found.

After some days, towards morning, we occupied the village, in which the dragoons had been positioned up till then; it was immediately attacked by the French infantry and we scattered behind a three-foot wall in pairs. Our captain stood behind us on a hillock near a chapel. He shouted to me that I should lie down, but since the place was befouled I called back up that I could not lie down. The command was repeated, I answered in the same way. Now my nearest man was shot through the hand, so I cried 'Forwards! Whoever will,' and jumped over the wall, shot my rifle and put my bayonet on. Five or six followed me and with a 'Hurrah!' we fell upon the enemy, who immediately turned tail and left many people there, as our whole battalion broke through. When we had moved behind the wall again, the captain reprimanded me and said that this time it had gone well but I should not do the same again. We halted in the village until about evening; we had to collect wood from houses and broken wagons and light as many fires as possible, a deception that the French had often made before, but which we only used this one time.

When it had become dark we slowly departed in the direction of Burgos; I found myself at the outermost point of the rearguard. After two hours we discovered an English storehouse in which wine and rum barrels lay scattered, some mouldy bread and a packet of cod. I took some pieces of the latter in my pack and chewed it around all night from hunger. Towards midnight we marched close to Burgos, where we had to act quietly: we were not allowed to speak nor to cough; adjutants came frequently to our point to collect information and gave us orders concerning the march. Soon after midnight we came to a sunken road and heard a noise in it. I listened and was aware of German speech; while my comrades were marching above I went down, and found there drunken people: four soldiers and my friend Reichert from Hamelin with the big drum, the one who had gone through the adventure in Elvas with me.

'Heinrich,' I said to him, 'what do you have in your drum?'

'Look, Friedrich,' he replied, 'it is good that I have met you here, I have brought rum with me in the drum for myself and my comrades,' and thereupon he shook the rum in his drum. I took it away forcibly, cut the skin in two with my bayonet, let the rum run out and gave it back to him with the words, 'There Heinrich, you have your drum, I have poked up the rum, but if rum is your pleasure, make sure that you escape or the French will poke you up,' and pushed him in front of me. At first he was very angry with me but when he was told more calmly of the dangerous position in which we found ourselves I did not have to urge him to hurry any more.

By dawn we came to a temporary bridge made out of a baulk of wood on which a mule with a broken leg hung half in the water, every now and again it raised its head out of the river to snatch a breath. The beast distressed me and I cut its leg off, after which it swam away in the river. After some time we came to a highway on which a cask of rum stood, with the top end knocked out. I half filled my canteen, my friend Reichert had lost his canteen but he filled his cow's horn that he, like almost all of us, had prepared as a container. Some adjutants came up at the gallop and learnt from us that we were the last, at which one of them dismounted from his horse, overturned the cask and let the rum run out.

The Action of Venta del Pozo

Of all the KGL's actions, that of Venta del Pozo was one of its most heroic. On 23 October, French cavalry pressed Wellington's rearguard. A British light cavalry brigade under Major-General George Anson fell back and crossed a bridge over a stream twenty-two miles south-west of Burgos, but then fell into confusion and accidentally masked a battery of horse artillery. This enabled about 1,250 French horsemen to cross the bridge and begin a fierce mêlée. The British and KGL cavalry opposed to them were forced back, as they were slightly outnumbered, and some were already tired from the retreat. The situation was restored by the KGL light battalions, which formed the tail of the infantry and repelled a succession of French cavalry charges, thus winning time for Wellington's horsemen to reform.

It was early in the morning when we again came back to our battalion, which was halted near the highway in open ground. Here meat was issued and we brought it to a fire very quickly but at the same moment there came the order to strike camp; we turned our kettles upside down, fastened them to our packs and put our meat into our knapsacks. The 2nd Battalion marched back against the enemy and settled close to the highway in a deep dyke near a bridge over which the enemy had to approach. Scarcely were we ready to fire than we heard some way away a cavalry engagement, with loud calls and cries. Immediately some English cavalry came in a distressed procession, springing over the bridge, the people full of blood, some riderless horses, others with deep wounds and their bowels hanging out, and in an instant they were away, with French cavalry close behind them. But when the French were over the bridge we gave them so fearsome a fire with our rifles that they very rapidly turned back, all those who were spared our bullets. We immediately formed a square and dragged along our artillery while the French followed cautiously.

This lasted almost the whole day and it might have been five o'clock in the afternoon when we came upon houses to the left and right of the highway. We marched through them and behind them found our dragoons halted, who attacked the enemy cavalry nearby as soon as we had come near. I saw the flash of the swords, the tumult of horses and men and heard a terrible screaming. We had hardly disposed ourselves, the 1st Battalion on the right and the 2nd on the left of the road, than our dragoons chased through between us singly or in little troops, some of them in a sorry state. One dragoon had an NCO sitting in front of him; he had had his legs shot off and his splintered knees dangled on the horse. The dragoon asked for a drink, I sprang from my rank and offered my canteen, which he held out for the NCO to drink from and then galloped away. A cannon, which had only three wheels, scraped through between us.

Among those following was a cavalry captain whom my neighbour recognised as Herr von der Decken, who rode without a hat past a dragoon and cried out, 'Stand fast, German brothers. The curs cannot do anything to you.' Lord Wellington too came chasing up on his own, spoke a few words with our Commander Halkett and dashed onto a hill behind us to observe the more distant attack of the French cavalry. Among the last to gallop up was Captain of the Guard Kielpennig without hat or sword, near him was a corporal and close behind them were the French. Commander Halkett called them both to him, they threw themselves from the horses and we had to start firing. Kielpennig was quick in throwing himself from his horse into the dyke and escaped; we fired and the corporal and the approaching French cavalry regiment fell.

A second regiment threw itself at our square and was bloodily repulsed. A third regiment was set loose on the 1st Battalion but suffered a similar fate. Again a fourth regiment wanted to get rid of us but could not properly come at us because of the numerous horses and riders that lay heaped up in front of us. They swung round again after they had got a hearty greeting from us and many people lost their lives. Now there was suddenly a French officer's horse, shot through the nose, in the middle of our square, trembling in all its limbs; no one had seen how it had got there – in its death agony it must have leapt over us. Sergeant Mener had appropriated it since he was the first to grab the reins and took as booty twenty gold Napoleon coins from its kitbag.

The horse was shot since its wounds were considerable. Meanwhile the French riders had retreated to a nearby hill and stationed themselves there. With a triple salvo we forced them to move on again, and as evening drew on we withdrew peaceably with fife and drum.*

After about one and a half hours we halted, received a ration of rum and, freshly fortified, continued the retreat throughout the night without being bothered by the French. On this road we found many groups of Portuguese, five to ten men closely pressed together, wrapped up in their blankets, lying on the road. They could not or would not go further, as much as we urged them to and even used force, since the Portuguese are by nature a lazy and feeble people not in a condition to tolerate exertions as we are; they like best to lie on their backs and let the sun shine on their bodies.

When it was day we came over a bridge and proceeded into a camp just left by the English, where we, at the command of Lord Wellington – who had praised our cold-blooded bravery on the previous day to our commander – were issued with two rations of wine, which we warmed on the still-burning watch fires. Not satisfied with that, some of us went into a neighbouring village, broke into the wine cellar and went for the best wine; I brought back a big kettle and several canteens full. We had not drunk it all, it might have been shortly before dawn, when a French cavalry regiment sprang on us over the bridge. Behind them the bridge flew up into the air, we opened fire and our cavalry

---

* Fife and drum marked a successful engagement. Venta del Pozo was counted a battle honour for the battalions.

93

suddenly came forward from an ambush, which had not been noticed by us, and cut the enemy down. The retreat was now very hastily begun again and we marched the whole day without being disturbed further. The following day, though, we had to deal now with the French infantry and now with the cavalry, but few of us were killed by them, for our officers led us excellently and we carried out the commands punctiliously. A great number of the enemy, who always came on in masses, were struck down by our bullets. To make the French retreat more difficult we had to destroy all the bridges we came across as we were the last in this retreat.

'THIS RETREAT WAS A MOST MISERABLE ONE'

Wellington had to retreat more than two hundred miles, all the way back to Ciudad Rodrigo and the Portugese frontier, which he reached on 19 November, almost a month after leaving Burgos. Discipline in many units disintegrated in the latter stages, following the onset of heavy rain and the temporary breakdown of the army's logistics.

Wellington lost about three thousand men in the retreat, and thousands more who had to enter hospital. On 28 November, he issued a memorandum to his generals, which criticised the disorders. This caused bitter controversy, not because the comments were entirely unjustified, but because Wellington tended, when angry, to issue blanket rebukes instead of directing his ire at specific units. Many of his subordinates also thought that he had mismanaged the siege of Burgos, partly because he had made piecemeal attacks in a misguided attempt to limit casualties.

Nonetheless, the 1812 campaign had been a partial success. Wellington had permanently altered the balance in the Peninsula. He had established a moral supremacy over the French in battle, proven his mastery as an attacking general, and not simply as the defender of a position, and forced the French to abandon southern Spain.

The enemy harmed us very little, yet this retreat was a most miserable one since we had rain and snow from above, strong cold winds and impenetrable mire so that we regularly sank over our ankles. All this was bearable so long as we were marching or were harassed by the enemy, but if we had to make a halt our knees shook and our teeth chattered because during the whole retreat our bodies were not dry and our shoes were full of water and mud; there was little to eat, cooking was impossible. Even worse off than us were the poor Brunswickers, who were near us all the time, and they froze in their linen trousers even more badly than we did. All this time I felt well, I was just angry that we continually had to fall back before the enemy, who might well think that we were afraid of them, which was by no means the case. If it had depended on our battalion we would not have let ourselves be driven back even one foot by the whole of the French army; but the commands of the superiors must be obeyed by the soldier, even if against his will.

One evening the order was given to cook; it was difficult for us to kindle a fire since it was pouring with rain and the ground was an endless morass, we got a large pile of wood together and succeeded in lighting a fire. As there was no water and in the whole locality there was nothing but mud we cut sticks from green trees and roasted our meat on them. Then I went to my brother who looked after the butchery for the officers' mess and asked him for a blanket for the night from the mules, but since these were not allowed to be unpacked, he could not give me one. I must also see, as I was ready to, that I had not unfastened mine, if I might, and that I would be better off frozen than spend the next days carrying my pack with its intolerable weight of sodden blankets.

For a long time I stood in front of the watch fire and roasted in front while I froze behind; then, since standing a long time was a considerable strain, I got a bundle of twigs together, laid it close to the fire and lay down bad temperedly on the ground by the fire. I must have slept a good hour when a violent pain in my feet woke me up. The fire had come near to me, my shoes were steaming and had so tightly shrunk that I could scarcely manage to get them off my feet and had to throw them away. I took my second pair of shoes from my pack and pulled them tight on my feet because otherwise the next day they would be left behind stuck in the mud. Several of my comrades now marched with one shoe; they had no others.

When we marched into a wood the following afternoon and heard some shots ahead and to the left of us, the word went round our company that there were pigs there. I promptly hid myself from the ranks and remained behind as far as the end of our rearguard, which was commanded by Corporal Dörge, a fellow countryman and a good friend. He asked me where I wanted to go and when I had made known to him my intention, he at once went with me. After we had gone a distance we saw one of our people sitting on the ground doing his business in which one does not readily interfere. Nevertheless six French cavalrymen sprang out on him and our comrade got a hard blow across the face but stood up quickly, pulled himself together, placed himself behind a tree, shot a Frenchman from his horse and ran as quickly as possible to our battalion. Meanwhile the French had turned towards us, but dashed away again quickly after I had shot one of them. Then we saw many more enemy cavalry in the distance so we thought it best to turn back quickly, even without a pig for our battalion, which had already halted and set the rifles in formation, since the French cavalry had been so audacious as to attack our baggage that marched in front of us.

But for the whole day we did not encounter each other; in the evening when it was already somewhat dark our two battalions, which formed the rear point of the retreat, reached a moderately wide river. We were wet through from the rain, yet in spite of that no one wanted to go through the river and there was no bridge near. While we were standing in front of the river and hesitating we suddenly heard close behind us cannon fire, which drove us as quick as lightning into the water. We held our rifles and cartridge cases, which we always treated with great care, high up. On the other bank, which was very steep, we first lifted some of our people out of the water, they then helped us to get to the land so that in perhaps five minutes both our battalions were safe from the pursuing enemy. Meanwhile the artillery continually fired at us but the shots went too high and only a few of us fell.

Now safe from the cavalry who were perhaps pursuing us, our company, which was the first ready to fire, let go a salvo against the cannon and at once silenced them. For a while we remained standing but the cannon did not touch us and as it had already become dark, we marched back for a short quarter of an hour towards our lines, which were in a big field, where we lay down with our rifles to hand. It had become very cold, though, and I saw a fire burning nearby in a low-lying meadow so I went there to fetch a firebrand for our watch fire. Just as I was going to grasp it a bullet flew from the French guard into the meadow, sending up sparks and cinders all around; so I headed back to where I had come from very quickly and without any fire: better to freeze than to sacrifice the lives of myself and my comrades to French bullets for the sake of a fire. Towards eleven o'clock at night, when we were already quite stiff with bitter cold and the perpetual pouring rain, a ration of rum was handed out, which I hardly wanted, I was so weak and disheartened. From here on the French did not follow us any further, but the last days of the retreat were no less wretched because the weather and the road were so dreadful.

One day, when we almost continually had to wade up to our knees through a morass, I was the witness to a sad event. A Brunswicker soldier, with two of his comrades, carried his wife who had just been delivered of a baby boy in a blanket with the morass below and the perpetual rain above – it was a piteous sight. It appeared that the people would not have the strength to carry the moaning woman to a house about a quarter of an hour away so I took a corner of the blanket and dutifully helped. We reached the house, quickly made a fire, both Brunswickers gave up their blankets and so we left the man and his wife to their fate as we had to hurry further to rejoin the march again and had been left a good distance behind them. Some weeks later I saw the man and his wife again; the child had died. They had fallen into the hands of the French, but were humanely treated and set free again when the woman had recovered.

On the evening of that day I remained with our out-post, under the command of Captain Holtzermann, in front of a little river, while our battalion encamped on the other side of it. Our sergeant ordered me to go through the water to fetch some meat and said that I should not remain on duty through the night. I crossed the river and came to the butchery, where I found my brother who gave me my meat and also gave me a tail end on which he had left an excellent chine. As well as this I asked for an ox hide, which my brother carried to the water for me. Here I first carried the meat over, cleansed my tail piece in the water and immediately put it in a kettle of water on the fire, then I also fetched my ox hide that lay on the other bank. When I saw that the soup was ready I asked my captain whether he would like a cup of broth. 'You always have a joke in your head,' he replied, 'where would you get soup now, since the meat has not yet been shared out?' However, he enjoyed the cupful of soup that I passed to him. He then asked me what I wanted to do with the ox hide. 'That will be my bed for tonight,' I replied, 'and I will sleep excellently in it, I do not need to describe that.' When I had lain in my hide for a while my sergeant, whose name was Schmidt, asked me how it went with me. 'I am very cosy,' was my reply, and he could share my bed since there was room for two in it. He crawled in with me and we slept the whole night in pleasant warmth and were only occasionally woken by the relief, since the sergeant had to get up, but he instantly sought out his warm bed again, his teeth chattering with the frost. On getting up the next morning we smoked our whole bed as a watch fire and it got so bad that we had to put it in the river at once.

That day we retreated to Rodrigo, where the winter quarters were. Here things went really well for me: I helped my brother buy pigs and slaughter them, we made sausages for sale and from that, even if there was no money left over, we always ate plentifully. At night we went in secret to the wine cellars that the peasants of that region keep in the mountains far from their houses. The peasants often kept watch but part of the time they were on their guard at meeting us, since they feared our fists, and part of the time we were on our guard at meeting them, since we feared an inquiry. For the whole winter the supply of bread and meat and wine did not fail, in addition we knew how to obtain chestnuts from the lofts of the peasants and hens from their coops. Only in England did we have a better life than in these winter quarters. So we were happy, as things continued; although we knew that only dangers and privations lay ahead, we still hoped that we would get through these hardships and return to our beloved native land. I did not much like the life in Spain: the people hated us and called us heretics and we had no desire continually to risk our lives for these wretched people and this inhospitable land.

5

THE VITORIA CAMPAIGN
1813

Wellington used the six-month winter lull to hone his army into a formidable fighting machine. It was, in fact, the longest period of rest his troops had during the entire Peninsular War. He now had 21,000 Spanish troops directly attached to his army, following his appointment as generalissimo of the Spanish armed forces. As part of the re-organisation, the two KGL light battalions were transferred in December 1812 from the 7th Division and joined three of the line battalions in the 1st Division.

Napoleon, meanwhile, had suffered a disaster when he invaded Russia in 1812, and he withdrew troops from the Peninsula to help form a new army in central Europe. Wellington was able to take the offensive in May 1813, and turn the French northern flank, hustling them back before they could concentrate, and sweeping right across Spain up to the city of Vitoria.

Then, on 21 June, Wellington wheeled round and fell on the French army in four separate prongs and heavily defeated it in the Battle of Vitoria. Lindau and the 1st Division were with the outer prong of 20,000 men under Sir Thomas Graham, which descended from the

north-west to try and cross the Zadorra river and cut the
French line of retreat to the east. Graham attacked at
three points, with the KGL light battalions being sent to
clear the innermost point, the village of Abechuco, just
over one mile north of Vitoria.

Lindau claimed that Wellington personally ordered
this assault, but was clearly misled by his memory, for
Wellington actually directed the battle from further
west. The light battalions took Abechuco with the loss of
fifty-two officers and men, and took several guns.[12] But
they were not, in fact, ordered to press on and attack the
bridge over the Zadorra further south, and so the fighting
was then limited to artillery fire. It seems that Graham
overestimated the size of the French forces opposed to
him, and followed Wellington's orders too literally to
synchronise his moves with those of the more westerly
prongs. Graham's troops crossed the bridge only after the
French defenders had retreated.

Thus, although Graham managed to cut the main road
to France, he could not sever the lesser escape route east of
Vitoria. Nor was Wellington able to mount an immediate
or relentless pursuit, partly because, as Lindau graphically
describes, much of his cavalry was more interested in
looting the French baggage. Indeed, the 18th Regiment of
(Light) Dragoons (Hussars) was subsequently disgraced
for its role in this pillaging.

Lindau mentions that he received a sabre cut from a
French cavalryman in the battle. It was, in fact, a serious
injury, and the incident was later cited when he was
awarded a pension for his wounds.

Battle of Vitoria

After some weeks we met the enemy, who withdrew into the region of Vitoria in uninterrupted flight in front of us, without putting up serious resistance. The enemy occupied themselves so little with us that we never had to fight against hunger as much as we did now, since the French destroyed or damaged everything on their retreat, and so we were lucky if we could pick up from the ground some beans or lentils that had been scattered in the cooking in one of the deserted French camps.

At dawn on the morning of 21 June near us on the mountain to the right we heard the roar of cannon and saw powder smoke. Our officer told us that the Spanish army was already in battle with the French; we should hold ourselves ready and set our rifles in position. Today we would drive the French into a corner. We set out and had to march for some hours but since we had not eaten or drunk the whole day we felt so weak that we could scarcely carry on, and some of our people remained lying on the road unconscious. About midday we saw before us a bare hill on which our general staff had halted; from there, as we were soon to discover, they could look over the whole French army, which was drawn up in the valley opposite. It was here that from time to time our commissaries came galloping up with some loaves they had extorted. Some three or four times our captain got a loaf of the size of a three-groschen loaf, he then walked around the company with it and for everyone, so far as the bread stretched, he cut off a little piece that, although it was little, filled us with new courage. When we had come to the foot of the bare hill Lord Wellington galloped up to us and cried to us from a distance, 'Half of each battalion are to go forward for the storming of the bridge.' The first four companies from our battalion and the four last companies of the 1st Battalion immediately moved to the right on the highway. I was heartily glad that we would be fighting the enemy properly again, and said to my neighbour, 'Now we must really take them to the brink, we have them again.'

Our first company went forward, but we were scarcely round the mountain when we saw the bridge in a hollow, obstructed by an abatis of thick trees with four cannon mounted behind it; a rattling hail of grapeshot immediately greeted us. We had already dispersed as skirmishers, though, and the bullets frequently hit the stones in front of us, so we suffered little, but looked at each other questioningly since there was such a smell of burning here that we thought our clothes were on fire. Behind us there was the cry 'Forwards!' and with a 'Hurrah!' we tore into the abatis and climbed over it, because we were not able to get through it. From the upper branches of the trees we brought such heavy fire on the artillery that the enemy pulled away with one cannon but the rest they left to the bayonets and made off with their horses, having cut the traces; the infantry who should have covered the cannon were also wounded. Eight of us, of whom one, Düwel, now lives in Gellersen near Hamelin, hurried from the abatis on to the bridge; we rushed on to the cannon on the left (which I had not seen from the two cannon on the right), overturned them and forced open the limber box since we hoped to find some bread in it but sadly only found a roll of tobacco. Immediately we eight skirmishers pressed forwards and shot at the enemy infantry that were stationed on the left of the highway. Suddenly cavalry faced us; two cavalrymen broke free towards me and I shot one at some fifteen paces; the other cut at me with the words: *'foundre couyon Anglais!'** I parried with my rifle and cried, *'foundre couyon Français!'* The Frenchman cut down at the barrel of my rifle and cut the knuckle of the index finger on my right hand but at that moment I did not feel it. Now he turned his horse and I thrust towards him but to no purpose; then he came to me on the right side since he must have feared the point of my bayonet, and forced me to parry his cut with my rifle butt held high; in so doing he wounded the bone of my elbow and cut deeply into the brass of my butt. When he once again turned I sprang towards him and stabbed him from his horse. Now I hurried to my comrades, of whom some had apparently fallen, since only six had come together as our common defence. Five of us formed a square and from the middle two shot down several cavalrymen who were constantly set against us, but always wheeling round again at a certain distance out of respect for our bayonets. Had our dragoons not been there we would not have survived five more minutes.

As our battalion advanced over the bridge we closed ranks and the enemy hastily retreated. We marched left along the river and here an English cavalry regiment that had already been in Vitoria rode by us. The people offered us money and when we told them that they certainly might throw it over, they dipped into their full breadsacks

---

* 'Sod off filthy English.'

and threw Spanish thalers to us, and in the crowd that had gathered I managed to catch some of the coins. Another cavalry regiment that followed the first and was loaded with looted bread and ham appeased our hunger. When night fell we lay down in open country and slept soundly after all the excitements of the day.

Action at Tolosa

Two days after Vitoria, Graham was sent to intercept the retreat of a French corps under General Foy, who had not been present at the battle. On the 25th, Foy made a stand at the walled town of Tolosa, thirty-five miles north-east of Vitoria. He had 16,000 men and occupied a strong position in a defile. Graham, with 26,000 troops, sought to evict him with a combination of a wide turning movement and a general attack. The main assault was spearheaded by the 1st Light Battalion – as the more senior of the two KGL light battalions, it typically led the way. But it was bloodily checked by the town's strong defences, and a cannon gun had to be brought forward, with the 2nd Light Battalion in support, to break down the gate. Foy retreated before he could be cut off and escaped during the night. The KGL suffered unnecessarily heavy losses because of the flawed planning of the attack: its five infantry battalions in the 1st Division lost 147 officers and men killed or wounded.[13]

The next morning at dawn we pursued the fleeing enemy into the mountains, but did not fire the whole day, although we heard cannon fire and small-arms fire to the right and the left of us in the mountains. Only occasionally did we meet with the enemy in earnest; once he wanted to take position in a vegetable garden, but was chased out by us. Another time he attempted to halt in a copse but was driven on by us with blows from rifle butts.

One evening we came near to a town; we received the command to hold ourselves ready for storming and were posted behind a wall close by. When the fire that the town garrison aimed at us had mitigated somewhat we stormed in front of it and came under a heavy rain of bullets under the gate, which was made of strong planks and was firmly closed so that we tried in vain to lift it off its hinges. Some of us shot up towards the wall from where we were being steadily fired on, but the firing ceased at once when our people brought up a cannon that burst open the gate with a few shots. When our battalion rushed into the town the inhabitants put lights by the windows and greeted us with cries of joy, but we hurried at the double through the town and on the other side met our own people, who had marched around the town. Nothing more was to be seen of the French, we only heard the fleeing troops in the distance and pursued them with a few shots. Then darkness set in, making us disordered and we did not dare pursue the enemy any further. Everyone was shouting to one another, one shouted for his battalion, another for his company. Our irritation increased when we were suddenly shot at from the side, which turned out to be the perfidious Spaniards, who had left us to the bayonets at the storming and remained quietly standing on the hill and now had taken us for French. After our buglers had blown a signal, the fire ceased, we sorted ourselves out again in rank and file and lay down to sleep where we were.

Perhaps a day's march beyond this we came, one midday, to a harbour that stretched wide across the landscape. The enemy infantry stationed in front of us tried to escape through the water; we were dispersed as skirmishers and I had a grenadier in front of me who did not look as if he was going over. I shot at him, he replied to my shot; it took a second shot to stretch him on the ground. I ran to plunder him, but found only a few copper coins in his pocket and turned back to my people. Soon after that I had the luck to shoot a pig dead near a house. My comrades cheered me when I dragged it on its back; very quickly we kindled a fire and several set about the pig to prepare it for cooking. Meanwhile I went out again for provisions with some others; we found six geese, cut their throats and came back to our company with this rich booty. We then gave the pig to the 2nd Company, having cut off a ham, we plucked our geese so that feathers flew up to our ears, cooked and roasted them all through the night and allowed ourselves to enjoy them. Next morning Captain Lindam thought that we had emptied people's beds for some mischief and wanted to scold us*; but when he saw what we had celebrated with for a feast, he was pleased and was happy to sanction it. Now I was sent with six men to the harbour to see if it was possible to cross it; we found the water was very

---

* They were up all night cooking when they should have been getting their rest.

shallow and waded through it in order to get booty from the village on the other side. French cavalry chased us away again, however, and we hurried back to report to our captain. Our cavalry immediately crossed through the water, with us behind them; but the enemy had already gone.

THE SIEGE OF SAN SEBASTIAN

Attention now shifted to the fortress of San Sebastian, which lay on the Spanish coast, fourteen miles north of Tolosa. Following Vitoria, Wellington had driven the French armies back to the Pyrenees, but now needed to consolidate his position before advancing further. That meant taking San Sebastian and the fortress of Pamplona forty miles inland, while using the rest of his army to cover the operations.

An initial attempt by Graham to storm San Sebastian failed bloodily on 25 July. At the same time, Wellington's army had to repel a French counter-offensive through the Pyrenees, which was aimed at relieving Pamplona.

Graham tried again at San Sebastian at the end of August. The previous attempt had been made by the 5th Division, and this time Wellington asked for 750 volunteers from three other divisions to spearhead the assault. Two hundred of these volunteers came from the KGL battalions of the 1st Division, and Lindau was one of them.

In the event, the volunteers were used in a supporting role, rather than as a forlorn hope, on the insistence of Lieutenant-General Sir James Leith, the new commander of the 5th Division. Lindau found himself deployed in the trenches as a sharpshooter to cover the storming force. The assault was planned for 31 August, and the volunteers entered the trenches under the cover of darkness. As Lindau describes, they had to spend the long hours of the morning waiting tensely. The assault was scheduled to begin at 10.55, for it depended for success on low tide to enable columns to cross the Urumea estuary.

The explosion that Lindau mentions during the early stages of the assault was a mine detonated by the French. It was less effective than intended: it killed only twenty or thirty men, as most of the storming troops bypassed the spot as they moved along the sands. Even so, the assault was initially checked on the breaches, so Graham boldly directed artillery fire over his own men, and onto the defenders. By now, Lindau and his fellow volunteers had come forward and joined the fighting on the breaches, and he vividly describes how he instinctively ducked for cover as the artillery shots passed overhead.

This supporting fire cleared the way for a renewed effort, and by 14.00 San Sebastian had fallen. As often happened during a storming, men half-crazed by the horror on the breaches began to sack the conquered town. The citadel on the height above held out for another week, but was bombarded into surrender on 8 September.

The fact that Lindau had volunteered for the storming of San Sebastian was later mentioned in his citation for the Guelphic Medal, a decoration introduced in 1815 to reward Hanoverian soldiers and NCOs who had distinguished themselves in the field.

After a few days we came in front of the fortress of San Sebastian and for some time stayed in camp behind it.

We had spent about fourteen days lying there when the demand was made that two volunteers from each company should come forward for the storming. I knew then that I was on sentinel duty and thus would be ordered up if no volunteers came forward, so I at once said to my captain, 'I am going with them.' Then I asked one of my good friends to go with me; he was called Degener, he was a shoemaker too and lived some hours the other side of Hanover, if I am not mistaken, in Langenhagen; I had seen him in the market in Hanover some years before. But he said, ' You know well enough what happens in a storming, I don't want to.'

'Why not?' I asked, 'It is also possible that we will come out of it well; if it turns out badly, it is all the same; if we get inside we can find fine booty.'

'Yes,' he said then, 'if you are going with them I will too.' The captain noted our names down and said that we should hold ourselves ready. The command to leave came at once and thirty-two men from both our battalions under the leadership of Captain Wynecken of the 1st Battalion – who now, as colonel, commands the bodyguard – marched off in the direction of San Sebastian.

Towards evening we lay down in an area planted with apple trees. While we were refreshed by the sweet fruit of these trees, volunteers from the whole army that lay in front of the fortress approached from all sides. Around midnight, when it was pitch black, after a short march we reached a chapel that was lit up and in which there were many beds ready, probably for those who were wounded in the storming. In this chapel we were told that soon we would come up close beneath the fortress, where we had to avoid making even the slightest noise. Then we crept one by one through a small breach in the wall and reached a trench in which we lay down. Although we thirty-two of both light battalions with our captain were pressed closely together our teeth chattered from the frost, it was so cold that night. Meanwhile everything around us remained quiet; only now and then did we hear high above us the relief of the French sentries but saw nothing. When at first it began to become light, we saw that we lay in a trench five feet deep and six feet broad, in front of us was a rampart manned with cannon, to the right near us were other trenches in which people also lay. When it became light a cannon was fired off every now and then; our tension mounted each moment, and the long nervous inactivity began to be irksome to us. As the sun rose higher our position became unbearable since we could not protect ourselves from the sun and the heat became overpowering; we drank a mouthful of rum, but that only increased our torment. We dare not move and in that way our tedium grew as we listened to the bells in the city striking the quarter hours high and clear.

At last, at about eleven o'clock, an English officer crawled into our trench with the order that we should fire heavily on the nearest battery as soon as we saw a cloth waving. Scarcely had the bells in the city begun to strike eleven than we saw a cloth and in an instant our cannon thundered against the fortress so that the earth shook. At the same time small-arms fire crackled out of the trench. We stopped the artillerymen who came in front of the shutters of the cannon up above and thus prevented the operation of the artillery as far as we could. A hundred yards to the right of us were Englishmen and Scotsmen storming against the rampart and there was a massive clamour of men and powder smoke. This uproar raged for two hours, the cannon crashed so fiercely that I could barely hear what my neighbour was crying out; then I heard on the right of us a muffled crash in the ground. I saw over to the right of us the front rank of the storming party flying some twenty feet into the air in a thick cloud of smoke, the remainder ran back in confusion. At the same moment Captain Wynecken ordered 'Forwards!' We stormed out of our trench to the right, over a pile of rubble of stones, earth and mutilated bodies against the fortress. Here a dead English officer lay by a big stone with his grinning teeth and a fearful expression on his face, still holding his sword in his outstretched hand – a sight I have never forgotten. Then through the thunder of the cannon that roared against the fortress from the English battery – so close above our heads that at times we instinctively ducked – we heard the muffled roar, close in front of us, a muffled thunder, and once again the earth flew up. We were covered by a thick cloud of smoke, but marched at the double over the smoking clods and reached the wall that surrounded the inner rampart of the city.

Ahead and twenty feet below us we saw a very small street that ran up to the wall and was full of Frenchmen who kept up so heavy a fire on us up above that we dared not attempt the edge of the wall. We could look down on the broad main street of the town in front of us, which was heavily manned and from which, as I observed, a constant successful fire was aimed at us. We immediately moved rather to the left until the bullets could not reach us any more. In the frenzy to stay here, we broke stones out of the wall and flung them on the heads of the French situated beneath us. That gave us some relief. I, together with my friend Degener, must have thrown down five such blocks of stone, when the French beneath us scattered. We moved further left and found a rise on to the rampart; we immediately stormed down it and our ten men broke in, shooting against the French who had crowded together in front of the main street, which was cut off by barrels filled with earth and stones. The crowd might have numbered thirty men, but we still went forward at it with fixed bayonets; I ran through the body of the nearest with my bayonet and, crying out '*Mon Dieu, mon Dieu!*', he fell down. We called out to them, 'Throw your weapons away!' They did so and came up to us calling out, '*Pardon, Monsieur!*'* We allowed them to pass between us and those who were storming up behind us took them back. We now noticed in the middle, between the barrels, a little slanting opening that could only accommodate one man, through which the French had pulled back into the main street, and from where the bullets rattled against the barrels as if ten partners in a nail smithy were in full activity. Whoever risked going through the alleyway was immediately shot though by a multitude of bullets, so we climbed onto the barrels, which were in three rows, one on top of each other; and when we were through the first row we were covered as though by a parapet and fired briskly on the enemy. As soon as a good crowd of our people had come together behind us, to support us, we advanced. With our

---

* In other words, 'I surrender.'

greater numbers we pushed with our combined strength against a barrel and succeeded in throwing it down on the other side. When we had thrown down four barrels we jumped over through the gap while our friends on the right and the left fired continuously. It is incredible to me, to this day, that none of us on the barrels was shot, but it was partly because we were standing tolerably covered and partly because the French in their great desperation shot very erratically.

We dispersed right and left by the houses and in the deep doorways of the houses tried take cover from the shots of the French, and shot continually at the thickly pressed crowd of the enemy that slowly moved backwards, as our troops increased every moment with the numerous Englishmen pushing in. After some minutes we heard the order from the barrels behind that we should press against the houses, since there was a cannon stationed behind us, but to take care since the people might pour boiling oil out of the windows on our heads. We then heard the crashes of some cannonshot, the balls roared away beyond us and knocked a gap in the crowd of Frenchmen; then hundreds of Englishmen stormed through the resulting opening into the high street. The French hastened in their retreat and we dashed in pursuit; but when another storming column of Englishmen pushed against us from a nearby street, the French cried '*Pardon!*' and threw their weapons away; they were taken back. We pushed further forward into a church that was full of French who asked '*Pardon*'; here we pressed on through to a little door through which the French had escaped to the citadel; when we got there it was shut. We left the church and had to stand in front of it in a crowd. Now I noticed for the first time that there was heavy firing from the castle; our battery replied to it with such a mass of shot that the earth under us shook. Here I met my friend Degener again; we greeted one another warmly and were glad that we were still alive and that the French had fallen back from the city. When we had stood here for a good hour, we were shown to a house, since it had become evening. On the way there I saw an open cellar and, almost raging with thirst, I plunged into it, found a cup, tapped it full and drank from it without noticing what was in it. I had drunk a good pint of vinegar. I could not breathe, I writhed with pain and dragged myself into the allotted house, where I soon became better, since wine had already been fetched. Although we had had a hot day and had not slept the previous night, we remained wide awake the whole night and recounted our day's experiences and drank the finest wine that was to be found in the cellar and rejoiced over the next day, when plundering should begin.

Towards morning the thunder of the cannon fire, which had been silent through the night, became stronger again and did not mitigate while we were in the city. With the break of day the plundering immediately began, a business that started without any orders. With my friend Degener I moved towards a big fine house but found the door locked. With the aid of a bullet through the keyhole it flew open. We found nothing here to detain us, though, so we burst open several houses in which we nonetheless found little. Then we came into a merchant's house and took booty of silver money, in another we found a shop, fully stocked. We each took an excellent bale of silk stuff of different kinds and colours and took them to our house, where already a corporal had been left behind to guard the many things hauled in. Then we came to another magnificent house, we climbed up the stairs inside, where we encountered several Portuguese, and in a fine room we found the body of a man, probably the father of a young woman who sat close by on a chair, held up by her mother, since her breast was pierced and blood streamed out onto her white dress. I took out a bandage from my knapsack, as we usually had two of them for people who might be wounded, and lifted up the young woman's arm. 'O *Signore, Signore!*' she said beseechingly; the older woman stood near as though petrified. I made a compress from the young woman's pocket, which was already full of blood, and bound it fast with my bandage while my friend held her arm up. While I was busy pinning the bandage tight some ten Portuguese came in and began to utter abuse: 'Wait now,' I said, 'Damnation take you! Degener, don't you hear what the fellows are saying? They abuse us as the devil and robbers; if this carries on, they are ill prepared and they are big-mouths. Draw your bayonet from its scabbard; we will cut them to pieces and give them trouble.'

'But there are a lot of them,' my friend protested.

'Just come here,' I replied, 'you shall see how the dogs take to their heels.' I was ready and drew my bayonet. We cut into the middle of them and it was their bad luck that they did not defend themselves, they all remained on the spot. With a loud cry and leaving behind a bloody trail they fell down the stairs; we pursued them as far as the door of the house. Then we went back to the room; the

117

old woman came to meet us with many expressions of thanks and praised the English in many words; we told her that we were German. She then fetched coins and in a low voice and with her hands clasped together asked us to remain. 'No,' I said to Degener, 'we don't want the money.' 'We want to get something,' he replied and then we hurried down the stairs and out of the house.

There were no inhabitants to be seen on the street, only soldiers who were dragging away booty or looking for it. When we went into the houses we found the inhabitants, who at once knelt down with their hands clasped, but nobody had money if we asked for it. We came to several houses without achieving our aim; in one we found a crowd of Englishmen in violent dispute, standing around an open chest. We succeeded in seizing money from a priest; his house had already been plundered and the utensils lay around in the kitchen, the chests of drawers and cupboards were shattered. In a long black robe with a girdle round his waist the priest stood in the middle of the room and received us with the words: 'The Englishmen have already taken everything away.' But in the kitchen we saw an undamaged chest of drawers and demanded that he open it. He refused. We took chairs and struck it, but the chairs smashed and the chest of drawers remained intact. The priest began to reproach us; then my comrade drew his bayonet and went for him. Then the man felt in his waistcoat pocket and put a key in the chest of drawers. We unlocked it and found linen, a big shawl with the Spanish coat of arms and a tortoiseshell box with gold edges and the portrait of the priest. When I had these two things in my hand he wanted to snatch them away from me but my friend Degener seized him from behind and threw him to the floor. As he did so he noticed that the gentleman wore a moneybag round his waist. We snatched this away forcibly and in it we found eight Spanish doubloons, and we each took four. 'Now we have money enough!' I said; we took the shawl and the box and went away. I gave the shawl to a soldier's wife, the box was stolen from me eight days later.

On the street we met my brother with a mule that he had got to fetch me since he had heard that both my legs had been shot off. I packed our silk stuff on the mule and my brother went back out of the city with it. Meanwhile, evening was coming on and we wrung food from the inhabitants, took wine from the cellars – there was such an enormous store of it that we would not have used it up in a week – and made ourselves comfortable in our house, where gradually all our comrades arrived and let us eat well. Then tiredness overcame us, we slept and were not disturbed by the cannonade from the citadel. The next morning at about eleven o'clock fresh troops were moved into the fortress, and we volunteers marched out of the city with rejoicing and singing, while the Englishmen took over the whole street and carried on all sorts of amusement of drunken boldness. They had wrapped ribbons thickly round their shakos so that the ribbon hung down to the ground; the man behind trod on it, the shako fell to the ground and was picked up again with swearing and stumbling. From time to time we halted and immediately slaked our thirst with the supplies we had with us, for each of us had some bottles of the finest wine in our knapsacks as well as our canteens. Thus we came staggering and rejoicing in front of the gate, outwardly and inwardly well charged. We parted from the Englishmen and marched to our camp some two hours away, without the cannon of the citadel, which were constantly put to work, becoming an irritation.

All of us who had been in the storming wanted our comrades to take a share of our booty; to my good friends I gave material for waistcoats and bought wine and rum from them since on the way we had already drunk the wine that we had plundered in San Sebastian. I began my sale the same day; the market women each bought some clothing; then crowds of peasants stormed into the camp. For a Spanish thaler (one and a half standard thaler) I measured off sixteen yards; I had seven pieces of material and each was seven hundred yards. I got such a mass of money that in the end the sale became a chore and I was glad when it finished. But, easy come, easy go. The money made me cocky; why should I save it? I did not know if I would be alive the next day. It soon went quickly out of my hands; not far from us lay the 2nd Line Battalion from which some people occasionally met with our people to gamble. I had never gambled but my brother was addicted to this passion and persuaded me to join them one evening. Five of us and five from the line met, amply provided with wine. We lit a fire in a copse, put the wine on it and sweetened it with sugar; then we spread kerchiefs on the ground and played for little piles of coins, from which we set a guinea on the card each time. The passion for gambling and the power of the wine eventually made us so intoxicated that we no longer knew what we were doing. Early in the morning I woke up near the fire, which had gone out, between my snoring comrades and broken bottles. I staggered to our camp and lay down in my tent. At about noon I was sober, counted up my money and found that I was poorer by two doubloons and some sixty thalers; I did not know exactly how much money I had had. I was so very angry over this gambled money, and particularly at the ridicule of my comrades and my wretched condition after the roistering night, that I vowed never again to gamble; I have kept my vow to this day. About a week later, when I heard that San Sebastian stood in flames, I took midday leave and went with some comrades near the burning town. There lay before us a great sea of fire from which thick columns of smoke arose; some isolated large buildings still stood, but the iron railings above were already becoming red hot from the heat.

'THE PIG IS OURS'

After some days we broke camp and marched into the mountains for a considerable time, but we did not seriously encounter the enemy, since they generally turned tail before us. I only remember one significant attack from this time. One morning at about ten o'clock both our battalions came into a wood of slender young trees that afforded no protection to us, and the leaves had already fallen. Many of these trees were torn to pieces by cannonballs and beneath them lay so great a mass of English weapons that we could have lit several fires with them. The butts had already been knocked off most of

them so that the enemy could not use them should the
weapons somehow fall into their hands. Among them lay
the bodies of many shot Englishmen and all the ground
was covered with blood. Here we were immediately
greeted by heavy fire from the French, who stood in front
of us in a wood of thick trees that was surrounded by
such a dense thorn hedge that we did not see the enemy
behind it, but could be hit by their bullets. Several of our
people were lost, although we immediately dispersed as
skirmishers. Our carpenters had to go forward at once
to cut gaps in the thorn bushes but were mostly shot or
wounded by the French. Meanwhile we succeeded in
crawling through in certain places and then, covered by
the trees, made an effective fire on the enemy, who moved
out of the wood after an hour and were then pursued by
us for the whole day. The next evening we were quartered
in a village, which was unusual for us. Our company was
in a big house that had a winepress. A large herd of sheep
immediately passed through the village, with a shepherd
leading; he trusted in our restraint and did not look round
once. But his trust was very much misplaced since people
came out from every house and took sheep; our company
took four as booty, which we very soon concealed in the
winepress under the apples, on which we eagerly began to
clean our belongings. Immediately the adjutant appeared
to carry out an inquiry and found us busily occupied,
making as much noise as possible over it and singing
heartily so that he would not notice if perhaps one of the
sheep betrayed us through its bleating.

As soon as our battalion was again stationed in a village
on the border with France I had further proof of the

cunning and cruelty of the Spaniards. We asked our host for wine but got the usual answer that he did not have any. Colonel Halkett was also quartered in the village, so we dared not use any force, and had to be satisfied with threatening our host with violence and frightening him. Probably to calm us down, he invited us to accompany him. He led us into a cellar, where from a corner behind two empty barrels he brought out two Frenchmen with their heads cut off and in triumph showed them to us and extolled his heroic deed. Then I said to him in a brusque voice, 'That's what will happen to you, if you dare do any harm to any soldier!' He tried to extricate himself from blame: his people had committed the murder, not he, and the French were good for nothing. The excuse was not accepted. If he did not now hand over any wine, I continued, I too would cut his throat, and at that I drew my bayonet. That helped. He spoke mollifyingly, led us through another door into the wine cellar and gave us wine. But he did not hand over enough, so he got a thrashing, with the threat that we would report him as a murderer. Then he begged for his life and promised wine, as much as we wanted to have, we had only to ask. We then had a cheerful night and our comrades in the neighbouring houses likewise.

It might have been about the same time that on one occasion we lay in open country and some of our people searched for wood. One man from our company returned looking cheerful with a bag full of wine, which we promptly set about and drank up. But we were still thirsty so we went together to the pit out of which our comrade had taken the bag and found around twenty bags with wine, enough to be shared by the whole battalion, so that each man had almost a full canteen – a piece of luck that was not often ours to share but which we valued very highly.

I prepared another treat for our company at this time. We were quartered in a village and I had noticed that a pig was kept in the cellar of a neighbouring house, with a flight of stone steps leading down to it. When it was dark I went to the house with my brother and another comrade; we fastened a piece of wood to both uprights and through the ring on the door, so that the peasant could not come out of the house, and while the other man stood on watch I went with my brother into the sty beneath the house. We had bought sulphur; we set it alight and wanted to suffocate the pig so that it would not squeal, but this did not work and so my brother took hold of the pig by the throat, which I cut with my blade. 'Ow!' cried my brother, 'you are cutting my finger off!'

'Just be quiet,' I said, 'and don't make any noise, the pig is ours.' I had struck lucky; we took it with us, cooked it the same night and shared the morsels with our company. The next morning the peasant must have been surprised to find his door barricaded and the sty empty. However, the peasants in that district could do without a pig, which had given them no hard work. When they harvest their corn they spread out it in an open place in the field, harness their mules to a board under which they have knocked in flints and on which they put a chair. In this way they go quite easily around the straw and the flints tear the corn from the ears. The winnowing of it was just as easy for them. To a fairly high upright they fasten a wooden funnel; they shake the corn down into this, and it slowly runs down through the lower opening; the wind blows the chaff away and the grain falls to the ground. The people make walking easy too. One day we came across a large herd of sheep with some shepherds, who moved around on stilts ten feet high, fastened firmly to their feet. In their hands they had a long staff. Our adjutant rode up to them and asked how quickly they could march with the stilts. He received the answer: 'An hour's march in a few minutes.' Then he asked one of them to go with him to the next town; the shepherd did so and our adjutant had to ride there at a gallop if he wanted to keep up with him.

6

THE INVASION OF FRANCE
1813–1814

———— ~⌇~ ————

Wellington's position was now more secure: he held San Sebastian, and the starving French garrison of Pamplona would surrender on 25 October. Napoleon was fully occupied in central Europe by the Russian, Prussian, Austrian and Swedish armies.

On 7 October, Wellington therefore invaded France by crossing the Bidasoa river. He did so at two points, near the coast and eight miles inland at Vera. The coastal thrust was totally unexpected by the French, who did not realise that the estuary was fordable. Wellington, who had learned from local shrimpers that it could be crossed at low tide, pushed the 5th Division across. To support it, the 1st Division crossed 1.5 miles upstream, at Behobie. It encountered stiff resistance until the French were outflanked by the 5th Division. The 2nd Light Battalion of the KGL lost forty-three officers and men killed or wounded.

A month later, on 10 November, Wellington attacked the French again, and drove them from their fortified positions above the Nivelle river. The 1st Division demonstrated on the western flank, and lost just 3 per cent of its strength, although Lindau's battalion was more heavily engaged than the other units and lost eighty-one officers and men, or 12 per cent of its total force.[14] Curiously, Lindau does not even refer to the battle, although his account of an evening attack on some houses and vegetable gardens may in fact be a hazy recollection of this engagement.

Lindau does record the small, wild horses, or *pottoks*, that roamed the Pyrenees in the Basque region. He also mentions one of the British army's more unusual regiments, the Chasseurs Britanniques. Formed in 1801, it eventually included not just French *émigrés*, or exiles opposed to the Revolution and Empire, but men from a wide variety of countries. It had a creditable combat record, but acquired a bad reputation for desertion, although this was partly the result of shedding large numbers of men during a limited, difficult period in July 1813.[15]

CROSSING THE BIDASOA RIVER

We were quartered in a village near the French border late one evening. I asked our host if he could provide wood and water and light a fire, but he was very insolent: he showed us the well and said that he had none of the necessities to provide for us. We had to look after ourselves and, since we had not received our rations, to see how we could get food because we were plagued by hunger. While some fetched water a fire was kindled. Others went to the peasant, spoke with him and held him fast in the room; the rest looked round the house for food. When they had found flour we cooked dumplings and roasted the meat

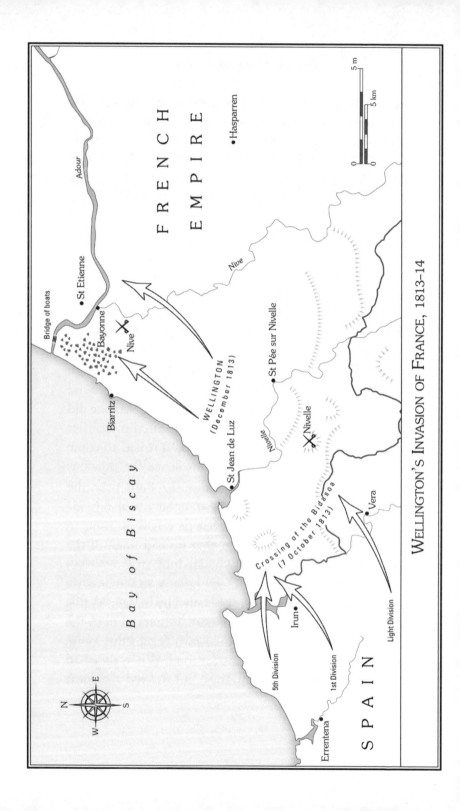

WELLINGTON'S INVASION OF FRANCE, 1813–14

FRENCH
EMPIRE

• Hasparren

Adour

• St Etienne

Bridge of boats

Bayonne

Nive

Nive

WELLINGTON
(December 1813)

St Pée sur Nivelle •

Biarritz •

St Jean de Luz •

Nivelle

Nivelle •

Vera •

Crossing of the Bidasoa
(7 October 1813)

Bay of Biscay

Irun •

Light Division

5th Division

1st Division

Errentena •

SPAIN

N
W   E
S

5 m

5 km

0

that had been provided in the meantime. We slept for some hours and we wakened before dawn and assembled in the middle of the village. When our battalion was ready to march Adjutant Riefkugel said to Colonel Halkett that it would be a good thing if we had a guide since it was still dark and we had to go through the water soon. So when the adjutant asked us if anyone knew a man who could show us a crossing point through the water, I stepped forward and said: 'In the quarters where we stayed there is a peasant who knows the way.' Corporal Weissleder, who had guessed my intention, stepped forward too and said the same thing. Some of us were sent to fetch the peasant. When he refused to go with us, we were glad that we were allowed to use force on him; we gave him a shove, none too gently and gripped him round his chest; he soon enough went willingly with us when he saw that his resistance did not help. On reaching our battalion the peasant said he did not know a way through the water. I repeated my earlier assertion and achieved my aim: the peasant had to come with us and was punished for his insolence the previous night. We had to move our battalion forward with the peasant and were commanded by the adjutant not to let him slip away. We waited for perhaps a half an hour at dawn on the river frontier; we ordered the peasant to go into the water first; he spoke conciliatorily – if we were quartered with him again we could drink as much wine as we wanted. That did not move us and when he still refused I moved him a little with my bayonet in his back and Corporal Weissleder said: 'You devil, we must teach you here how to get water so that, if Germans once again come to your quarters, you will wash better.' One could not blame our peasant for refusing since on the opposite bank there was a gently rising hill where batteries appeared to be stationed. Meanwhile our battalion was approaching; we went into the water, with our peasant shoved in front of us. From the enemy outposts on the other bank some muskets fired on us and the peasant ducked each time deep in the water. Corporal Weissleder, who now felt sorry for the peasant, said: 'We must let him go right under and then let him run.'

'No,' I said, 'he shall see us over the water, while the French shoot.' The water carried away some of our people, either shot or wounded, and we were scarcely on the opposite bank when we formed company lines. Now I could no longer delay the peasant, and I am sure that he would have made his way home very hurriedly, since the Spanish are fleet of foot when it comes to running away – something that I have been able to observe on a number of occasions.

We moved forwards slowly and replied to the fire of the enemy outposts; but first our whole battalion stood in line and then advanced quickly. Now the hill that lay in front of us was alive; a mass of infantry fired a salvo and with a 'Hurrah!' rushed against us. We fired once, drew our bayonets and ran with a 'Hurrah!' against the enemy, who had no desire to meet us in such proximity, but turned to flee in great confusion, like an ant heap, swarming over the mountain that lay in front of us. Major Prince von Reuss from his flank chased after the fleeing French, cut his way through them, turned back to us and cried, 'Forwards! Comrades, on to the dogs, then!' and then slashed away into the enemy. After half an hour we found ourselves not far from the summit of the mountain, from which we were continually fired on with small-arms fire; we replied with some shots upwards and turned left towards the summit, which was unoccupied, while we directed our shots to the right where the enemy were positioned. On reaching the top, we saw a plain in front of us, with the enemy already steadily retreating; we followed them for the whole day, however, our battalion forming the front and continually exchanging shots with the enemy rearguard.

One day towards evening we were very tired and saw not far ahead houses set in vegetable gardens where the French were holding fast. We wanted to spend the night there so together we moved nearer and attacked the enemy. By storming it we won the gardens and now, under cover of the thick trees, fired at the houses that the French had just left. Behind the houses in a hollow was a little stream where the enemy held out and fired heavily at us; we were again storming the hill behind when a signal called us back. While I was going back there was a grenadier still on this side of the stream, who showed no inclination to follow his fleeing comrades, and he shot at me from below. This annoyed me; I raised my rifle, laid him low and at once ran down to him. The man had a bullet through his breast, I searched his things but only found a little copper money and in his pack dirty washing, which I left alone, and hurried back to my comrades.

Now very bad weather began and for some weeks we occupied a camp in open country, which was by no means agreeable to us because we were bored and had to make do with our rations. One day we saw to the right in front of us on the mountain a herd of cows and sheep

and I at once agreed with some friends that we would
go out that night for booty. It was about midnight, the
moon was covered with clouds when we moved, fully
armed, out of the camp and began to climb uphill. We
searched for perhaps an hour; we found isolated houses
without stalls, but nowhere any herd. Then on a heath
we came upon a great herd of small, very beautiful
ponies, perhaps five hundred of them, without any
herdsman. We succeeded in chasing some thirty of them
to our camp; certainly several of them ran back again
between us to the large herd, but with a great effort we
forced about sixteen of them into a deep depression. I,
with my brother and another comrade, ran forward and
came into the hollow from the other side while the rest
forced the horses forwards. When we came near the
little animals they reared up and leapt at us with their
forefeet. But each man held one; I seized mine with
both arms around its neck, threw it to the ground with
myself on top of it so that its resistance did not help it
very much; my brother had not got hold of his properly
and was bitten by it in the elbow and cried out loudly
in pain. When the comrades on the other side, who had
let the rest of the horses jump out, hurried to help us,
his animal was thrown to the ground, so that it let go
of him, but his arm was black and blue for a good many
weeks afterwards. Now we tied up the mouths of the
ponies with our canteen straps, two of us seized each
one of them by its long mane and thus we led our three
wild ponies to the camp, where they were taken to the
mules, which had to carry the battalion's cauldrons and
tents, and tied up there. The next morning we had the

first proper opportunity to inspect our booty. Our ponies were black all over, they had manes and tails down to the ground, they were the size of a little donkey, glossy like an eel and round as a ball. If we came near them they reared up on their hind legs and opened their mouths wide, which looked so dangerous that we did not risk approaching them all day. But the next day, when they had already been hungry for nearly twenty-four hours, they appeared somewhat less wild; we tied them with long guy-lines round their necks, with the other ends fastened round a tree trunk and whipped them round the tree. After three days they let us stroke them, somewhat later we could ride them. When the officers asked us where the animals came from we said that they had been caught by us in the camp, the peasants would come to claim them back but we wanted to have booty money for them. After a few days I put a bridle on my horse and went for a ride alone; at the beginning it went very well but when I was outside the camp my horse became wild and took me through a green thorn bush that had very long thorns where I could no longer hear or see and soon blood ran down from my face, hands and legs. I made the horse stop in front of a high hedge; I jumped off, gave it a hearty thrashing and led it into a nearby camp where there were our troops of the line. Here a great crowd of people soon gathered around me, some officers came too and took a great liking to the little horse; one of them gave me four thalers for it. I took off my bridle, put my money in my pocket and, in spite of my injuries caused by the thorns, went cheerfully back into our camp, where I squandered the money with my comrades.

At this time I was stationed at an outpost on a rather dark night and held the outermost point; I found myself in a sunken road, to my right was a thick wood. It was quite quiet; only now and again did I hear a rattling in the wood and supposed that it was something wild, but I had the place well in my sight. Suddenly a man appeared. I fired and immediately I was fired on for perhaps half an hour by the whole French advance post line but I drew back, with my rifle loaded, under the cover of my number two man. The adjutant came to the principal outpost to find out what had happened, but when it had become quiet again I was taken back to my earlier post. The next morning, when I had the same post again, I saw a *chasseur Britannique* lying close to the sunken road in front of the wood and I learned then that he was a deserter who had tried to use the cover of darkness to go over to the enemy. These *chasseurs Britanniques* spoke French and were not well disposed towards the English but I was sorry that I had shot him dead; I would have let him escape if I had recognised him.

The investment of Bayonne

By advancing over the western end of the Pyrenees, Wellington arrived south of the French city of Bayonne. On 9 December, he consolidated his position by pushing his right wing over to the east bank of the Nive river, while his left wing advanced on the west bank to reconnoitre the approaches to Bayonne in strength. The KGL battalions of the 1st Division saw some fighting that day, and lost seventy men killed or wounded, but Lindau hardly mentions these events.[16]

Over the next four days, 10–13 December, the French under Marshal Soult launched a counter-offensive. Wellington had to repel a series of counter-attacks on either side of the Nive, but Lindau was not engaged, partly because the 1st Division had initially been placed well to the rear in reserve.

Lindau does record the mass desertion of some German infantry units serving with the French in the Peninsula. That October, Napoleon had suffered a disastrous defeat at Leipzig, which cost him control of central Europe and accelerated the defection of his German allies and satellite states. The 2nd Nassau Regiment received secret orders to desert, and did so on the evening of 10 December, when it marched into Wellington's lines, along with a Frankfurt battalion from the same brigade. Lindau refers to the Frankfurters as Primassers, since the Grand Duke of Frankfurt, Karl Theodor von Dalberg, was also the Prince-Primate, or *Fürst-Primas*, of the Confederation of the Rhine. Two years later, Lindau would find himself fighting alongside some Nassau troops while defending the farm of La Haye Sainte at Waterloo.

A lull ensued during the winter, although Lindau misleadingly gives the impression that the operations near Bayonne continued without a break. Then, in February 1814, Wellington took the offensive again, thrusting inland and drawing Soult's field forces off to the east. This enabled the detached left wing of Wellington's army under Lieutenant-General Sir John Hope to invest Bayonne and its garrison of 14,000 French troops.

Hope had a total of 18,000 men, including the 1st Division. He needed to push part of his force over the

Adour river between Bayonne and the sea, so he could invest the city on both banks. On 23 February, the KGL light battalions took part in feints south of Bayonne to distract the French from the crossing point. British troops were ferried across the Adour by boats and rafts. When a French column belatedly advanced against the bridgehead, it was thrown into disorder and induced to retreat by a shower of Congreve rockets, primitive and erratic missiles best used in salvos and against large targets such as besieged towns. Their unreliability did not impress Wellington, but they did occasionally manage to terrify opponents who faced them for the first time, as happened here.

On the 24th, a flotilla of boats sailed up the river from the Bay of Biscay, and was used to form a temporary bridge. By the afternoon of the 26th, the bridge was complete, and the next day, the blockade of Bayonne was tightened when the KGL took the village of St Etienne, one mile north of the city, in a fierce action that Lindau describes in detail.

The following days we had to move ever nearer to Bayonne since we had for a start beaten back and shot an unsupported sortie by the French; it did not come to hand-to-hand fighting since the French no longer had any real courage. Just after this sortie, at about ten o'clock at night, we received the order that we should be watchful since that night some regiments would cross over to us. I had the front point of the outposts and stood close in front of a swamp through which a narrow road had been made. It was about eleven o'clock, a starlit night and all around me was quiet – suddenly I heard on the other side of the swamp, where the enemy outposts stood, a great amount of small-arms fire and loud cries of 'Hurrah!' and soon afterwards two mounted officers burst in on me. I called out to them and received the answer in German: 'Good friend we are fellow countrymen and are coming over to you.' At the same time Adjutant Riefkugel and Colonel Halkett rode up and spoke with the officers; meanwhile two German regiments, declared by us to be Nassauers and Primassers, were marching over to us at the double. On the other side of the swamp we heard the shooting gradually cease, nevertheless our outpost was doubled and the greatest vigilance was ordered.

The next day we advanced through the swamp and came into a little pine wood but could not see Bayonne at all. Beneath Bayonne some of our companies were immediately sent over the river in boats; a bridge of boats was knocked up for the rest of us. The enemy did not trouble us on this crossing; if they had they would have paid for it dearly since to the right of us in front of a wood stood some rocket gunners. Each of these had three two-inch-thick shafts nine feet long in a triangle placed in the ground and bound together at the top; a three-foot chain hung down from the top of this stand. On the ground by each man there lay some twenty metal canisters, perhaps one and a half feet long and two inches thick, similar to a big clock weight. Of this devilish weapon I have heard much told, but I have never seen them in operation.

When we had arrived at the other bank in our boats Captain Wynecken from the 1st Battalion and his company swerved over to the right of us, away from the enemy; we

moved forwards in another direction and in a few hours
came across a highway and were quartered in a village near
it. While we were here we fed well on a peasant's chickens
– we were accused of this in front of the officer and the
matter would be investigated. A few hours later, of the ten
men who had stayed in the quarters, I was the only one
armed, most were dead, some were badly wounded.

The next morning when it was still dark we moved again
and at dawn were stationed between isolated houses. I was
posted on the left flank and had a highway near me on the
left; on the other side of it enemy skirmishers immediately
appeared and shot at us, but we returned their fire to
good effect because we were covered by the houses. We
had fired in this way for perhaps an hour when an enemy
column of perhaps one hundred men moved towards us
on the highway leading out of Bayonne. On the flank we
discussed what to do – the skirmishers were at our side,
the column came from in front. We withdrew, however,
and the houses fell under the control of the enemy, and we
later had the trouble of driving them away again. Because
of this, I advised that we should first draw the column's
fire and then attack them by storm.

This proposal was agreed; three of us immediately
stepped onto the highway, shot at the column and threw
ourselves to the ground as our fire was returned. At the
same moment we stormed the column; it was our section
of sixteen men under Corporal Steingrand, who now lives
in Hanover, who rushed against the column. Five yards
from the enemy we fired, which caused a great confusion,
then we stormed them with fixed bayonets. I stood on the
left flank, promptly ran my bayonet through the body of

the enemy officer with two golden epaulettes; the man collapsed in front of me. I seized his sword, which looked to have a golden hilt; my next man Düwel, the same man with whom I had stormed the bridge at Vitoria, tore away an epaulette from him. When the two men next to the officer abused us as '*couyons Hannovriens*' and tried to stab me I jumped left into the roadside ditch and struck out at both of them with my bayonet in their faces so that they turned away. My next man Düwel immediately stabbed and cut at the Frenchmen, one of whom tried to block a thrust, but I struck his weapon and ran through his side with my bayonet. The rest of my companions had also been active; the first rank of the French had been beaten to the ground by us, I stabbed down some of the second rank of them, too, and they turned to flight so that soon the whole column moved backwards and I saw how my next man Kuntze, whose home was in Hanover, similarly used his bayonet to pierce the back of the French who were now running in front of us in hurried flight.

But our joy did not last long. Some hundred yards further on, where our road converged with the highway that we had crossed the day before, the fleeing enemy suddenly turned left between some houses and at the same time we received cannonshot and a murderous small-arms fire from that side, where perhaps a whole regiment had halted. I saw my companions fall; I stood for a moment undecided then sprang over the highway in a few bounds, and just as I threw myself in the ditch my rear man, König, from Holland, fell on my body with the cry 'O God!' My friend, who had shared every danger with me for a whole year lay motionless beside me, he had a bullet through his head. When we entered Ostend later his poor mother came to us and asked after her son; she cried out and wept when she was told that he lay somewhere in front of Bayonne, and I had to give her a full account of how he died many times.

At the corner where the highways met, a very large Jewish cemetery lay between them, surrounded on all three sides by a nine- or ten-foot-high wall, but on the inside the wall was only four feet above the cemetery. Our battalion entered here and kept up a sharp fire on the enemy regiment, who returned fire with full volley. I loaded my rifle again and shot at the enemy that was sometimes standing only some twenty yards away from me. When they drew back some thirty yards after perhaps half an hour, I seized the opportunity to leap up and run to Corporal Steingrand, who was lying where the two roads met. He asked me to take him with me, but since my comrades were calling from the cemetery that I should come as quickly as possible because the French were already moving forwards again, I left him there and gave him my word that he would soon be fetched when we had driven the enemy back. I took some payroll money out of his knapsack that he, as he had told me, had got for us the day before, and hurried back to the highway. Just then my friends Düwel and Kuntze came out of the ditch that I had lain in; Düwel could move – he had a bullet in his arm – but Kuntze had been shot through the leg and hobbled along with the help of his ramrod and rifle; he leant on my shoulder and so we hurried on as fast as we could go as the enemy bullets again whistled past our ears. About a hundred yards from the end of the cemetery we

found an iron door; it was opened for us by our comrades
and Kuntze and Düwel lay down inside near the wall. I
hurried over to my comrades and we shot at the enemy
so assiduously that more cartridges had to be supplied
to us several times. It was very upsetting for me to see
my corporal lying without help and to hear him crying,
without being able to help him.

At one point the French tried to storm our wall, whereupon an enemy officer who had already climbed it was
seized by one of our people. Here indeed we took an officer
prisoner, and for a long time he ate with our officers in the
mess and I met him again later at Waterloo. When the
French had withdrawn behind the houses that lined the
street it was rather quieter and I noticed then that two
shots had gone through my hat, shooting off one of my
cockades, and that I had a slight wound on my forehead
and that some blood, which I had taken to be sweat, had
run down my face. Three bullets had hit my cartridge
case and were pressed, as flat as a thaler into the metal;
some bullets had torn my coat tails, another my knapsack
from which the payroll money had already for that reason
disappeared.

When it became dark, we left a garrison in the cemetery
and withdrew to the houses from which we had stormed
in the morning. Our company was stationed there in a
chapel, in the middle of which we lit a fire, for the flames
to protect us from the cold; we had nothing to cook, we
did not even have a little bit of dry bread. A hundred yards
behind, on the highway, stood a large house in which our
wounded lay; I went there that evening to visit my friends.
I could not find Kuntze and never saw him again since he

died some days later, but Düwel lay among a crowd of wounded men, who cried out and moaned, with his arm shot away and the splintered bone protruding through his uniform. In spite of the intense pain he was experiencing his first question was whether we had chased the French back, then he expressed his happiness that I had come out of it unscathed. He asked me to stay with him while his arm was taken off, but I only had a few minutes' leave and I was glad when I was out of that house of misery. After we had been supplied with new cartridges and a mouthful of rum, I lay down but could not sleep for grief, since I had lost my best comrades, and for the noise and smoke; I also did not dare take off my pack.

'THAT FELLOW WILL NEVER SHOOT AGAIN'

Wellington, with most of his troops, pursued Soult's field army eastwards, and inflicted two serious, but indecisive defeats: at Orthez on 27 February, and then at Toulouse on 10 April.

Sir John Hope's detached wing remained near the Atlantic coast to blockade Bayonne. Relations between the opposing outposts were relaxed, partly because Hope wrongly believed that the French garrison would soon be starved into surrender. Hence, as Lindau relates, the men were directed not to snipe at their opponents.[17] Despite this concern to avoid unnecessary loss of life, the blockade would end in tragedy.

On the following days when our battalion lay in camp somewhat to the rear, we had a rest, but also much aggravation when we were stationed as an outpost and when the enemy now and them shot one of us dead without our being permitted to return fire. Indeed in our camp two men from the 2nd Company were killed in their tent by a cannonball. We usually had our outpost in the Jewish cemetery from where I had seen my poor friend König lie in the ditch for eight days without being able to bury him. A large number of dead men lay there and it was so hot that they began to decompose and spread so disgusting a smell that we were glad every time we were relieved from the post. The body of a Frenchman, which had been in the Jewish cemetery for eight days and which had been looked at by many of our officers, did not degenerate into decomposition: his limbs were stiff but his face blossomed like a rose.

Meanwhile we had to stand in the trench to the right of the cemetery, where we had to be especially careful because this place was shot at most of all with long rifles from the citadel. In front of this trench towards the citadel there was a piece of cultivated land; I supposed that it was planted with potatoes, looked for them and succeeded in discovering a mealful while a number of shots fell on me from the citadel; they did not trouble me because my hunger was greater than my fear of death. Soon afterwards some Englishmen came out of the trench on the right and also looked for potatoes; two of them were immediately shot, the other ran back again. Another time I stood there as an outpost in a house in front of which and somewhat higher there was a flower garden. Behind this in a hollow stood the French outposts who talked to us in a sociable way from time to time and we both lied (since the French were also short of supplies) how good we had it and how ample our store of provisions was. One morning I stood at this outpost and conversed with the French opposite and went into the garden to pick some flowers, which the French did not stop me from doing. About three of them, who had crept up, immediately fired, the bullets whistled over me, but with one bound I was out of the garden and standing in front of the house, just as an English officer stepped out of it and gave me a strong rebuke.

At midday on the same day (my anger at the reprimand I got and the cunning of the French was still fresh in my mind) I said to Captain Lindam, who was at the outpost: 'It is not fair that we are not allowed to shoot at all and the French constantly fire on us if we put in an appearance.'

'It must not happen,' he said, 'it is strictly forbidden.'

'I will not refrain from shooting if I surprise one,' was my answer. The captain turned round and went away without answering me. So I believed I had a half 'Yes', took my rifle and crawled into the trench nearest the fortress; one detached house in front of it was occupied by the French. A French officer had shot at us from it from time to time for some days with a long rifle; I aimed at him. I had removed the round from my rifle, taken double powder, put in a ball with a patch on, and I lay down at the lookout after I had crawled a certain distance nearer behind a little mound.

I had lain there a good hour when the officer came to the window. He put his rifle in place and took aim; I pulled my trigger and in a moment saw, with indescribable joy, my man fall out of the window. I hurried back, but remained lying in the trench because I saw that our company had to form up. Immediately Adjutant Riefkugel and the brigade major came and held an inquiry, but they went away again when our captain told them that nothing had happened. When they had gone away I crawled out of the trench and got a reprimand from the captain. But when I looked at him and saw how glad he was that he had seen the officer fall from the window, I replied, 'That fellow will never shoot again.' After the surrender of Bayonne some Germans from the garrison came into our camp and asked who had fired at the officer; I was called in and then they told me that they had just sat down at the table in the barrack room, my bullet had pierced the dish and all their soup spilt upon the table.

THE SORTIE FROM BAYONNE

Wellington's operations formed just one element in the wider war against Napoleon. Britain's coalition allies, led by Russia, Austria and Prussia, captured Paris at the end of March, and Napoleon was forced to abdicate unconditionally on 6 April.

News of the abdication reached Wellington at Toulouse on the 12th. But the information seems to have provoked the French governor of Bayonne, General Pierre, Baron Thouvenot, into a final, futile gesture of defiance. In the early hours of 14 April, 6,000 French troops, or half of the garrison, made a sortie from the northern side of Bayonne.

Amidst the confused fighting that ensued, Sir John Hope himself was wounded. Nonetheless, the French were repelled, partly because Major-General Heinrich von Hinüber of the KGL used his initiative and counter-attacked from the eastern flank, driving the French out of the village of St Etienne. As a result, the sortie achieved nothing except waste lives. Lindau's battalion alone lost ninety officers and men killed, wounded or missing.[18]

Lindau gives the impression that Bayonne capitulated immediately after the sortie. In fact, there was only a temporary truce to collect the wounded and bury the dead. The governor refused to surrender for another fortnight, until after he received an official order to do so.

Shortly before the surrender of Bayonne we still had a hard fight. The report had come that peace had been concluded and our duty was lighter: the outposts were still regularly set but we no longer needed to stand formed up on the highway at night and in the daytime to carry fascines, a duty that we could not have borne much longer. We already hoped that hostilities were at an end and our work done, but one night, when our half-battalion stood on outpost duty, the rest of us in the camp were woken up towards morning. We immediately made a start under arms and heard strong fire on the other side of the city. It was not long before a fearful roaring of cannon broke out to the side, together with a furious shooting of small arms and loud calls and cries. We at once hurried at the double to help our outpost and drew up on the highway near the Jewish cemetery. It was here that Captain Wynecken of our battalion – who now lives as a pensioner colonel in Celle – one of our best officers, respected and loved by all of us, was to our great sadness carried off by us, severely wounded.*

Although we had not yet come right into the fight and our outpost stood some distance from us, we suffered a great deal from the grapeshot from the fortress because the enemy, who constantly threw wreaths of flaming pitch near us and among us, could observe our post very clearly. Single bombs, flying through the air like fiery wheels, also came down near us, burrowed holes in the ground and burst into pieces with a fearful crash. However, they did not do us any harm since some of us ran behind neighbouring houses and others threw themselves on the ground if such a monstrosity landed near us. When we were moved forward a little, the fire of our outposts, who stood in front of us in a hollow, slackened; then I heard the commander say, 'I don't know what that means, I can see in front our people lying in the hollow and they don't shoot.' Immediately Adjutant Riefkugel hurried forward through the shower of grapeshot, came back and brought the news that our people in the hollow were almost all killed.

Now we advanced at the double into this hollow, where we found Captain Holtzermann, who is now a colonel and town mayor in Hamelin, with the remainder of his

---

* When Wynecken was carried through the KGL lines after the battle the men gave him three cheers, a rare tribute from German troops.

company under heavy fire. Our arrival strengthened this post significantly, nevertheless the enemy infantry standing in front of us made an occasional attack, but never advanced up to our bayonets. Their attacks only served to give us some relief, since during them the fire of the grapeshot ceased, otherwise it whirred among us almost continually, like a flock of partridges. With the dawn the enemy drew back; the guns were silent and we could survey the battlefield around us. Friend and enemy lay mixed up together, the wounded moaned and begged for help.

We had stood to for a while in the expectation that the enemy would renew the attack when the white flag was hoisted on the highest tower of the citadel. It was now peace. The French had once again vented their anger but it had turned out to be a costly stance, for when we had to gather our dead some hours later the French had no fewer dead at our positions than we did. Then three holes of the size of the usual living room were made where we had stood; we packed in the dead in layers, each time spread quicklime in between and filled up the holes again. Rifles, bayonets, cartridge cases and packs were brought back; before this the wounded had already been taken on wagons to the field hospital. We stayed about fourteen days before Bayonne and it was quiet.

The fine hilt that I had taken as booty from the French officer was admired by my comrades; the officers themselves took it for a golden one; and for that reason our camp follower, who was a Jew, gave me twenty-two thalers for it, a sum that came in good stead to me and my friends since we had had no pay for a long while and my money from San Sebastian was long used up. Of course after some days the camp follower wanted to have his money back since the hilt was not gold, but I laughed at him – if he had been deceived then the French officer had also deceived me. However, my twenty-two thalers gave excellent service. The French came out of Bayonne to visit us, and I drew my purse out of my pocket, jingled it with a lot of money and ordered a bottle of wine to be fetched; I invited one of my comrades to do the same, after I had previously slipped him my purse with which he also swaggered; all the row did the same and the French were astonished at our wealth. One day a fellow countryman of mine came up. He was Junge, from Hamelin, with whom I had certainly served as a boy in the janissary band; he had allowed himself to be employed by the French, since he, as a tailor's apprentice to his master Nonne in Hamelin, had stolen a sausage and for fear of punishment had run away. Our way of life pleased him so greatly that he wanted to desert and come with us to England, but he did not put his resolve into effect.

Some days later I went into Bayonne, but it had to be stealthily because we were forbidden to do so, as our people had already had some brawls with the French in the city. Our adjutant's servant had lent me his clothes and as a precaution I fastened on my bayonet underneath. I entered without being stopped, went into the theatre and there met the wife of an NCO, the daughter of a foreman in Hamelin, who was very pleased to find a compatriot. After the theatre I went with her and her husband to a wine bar, where we chatted away for some hours with happy memories.

At about midnight I came out of the gate and hurried rapidly to the camp. As I went through a hollow, I heard the sound of horse's hooves behind me and, when it had come quite near, I moved to the side, but instead of a horse I caught sight of two Portuguese with sticks lifted up in front of me. 'What do you want?' I asked.

'You are a Frenchman,' said one of them.

'I am a German rifleman,' was my answer. At the same moment I spotted two Portuguese on the other side, so I stepped back a little to keep my back free. I would gladly have quickly drawn my bayonet, but I could not do so unnoticed since it was securely buttoned up; then one of the Portuguese asked me, 'Have you any money?'

'Yes,' I replied and unbuttoned my coat, but at the same time I bared my bayonet and gave one of the Portuguese a hard blow in his face and he fell down. I stabbed the second, who struck out at me, through his arm and he took to his heels, together with the two others. Then I struck the one who lay on the ground four hard blows with the flat of my blade so that he yelled out in pain and I made my departure.

Going through the hollow where we had stood in the terrible night and by the cemetery I reached my comrades. I would gladly have told them of my adventure since the villainous Portuguese whom I had marked so closely were certain to turn up again, but it was strictly forbidden to us to go into Bayonne and carried a penalty of three hundred lashes, and therefore I kept quiet. Some days later I went into the field hospital to visit my friend Düwel, but I asked for him in vain; I walked out of the inner door and saw lying there a mass of cut off legs and arms. I hurried away as if hounded.

From Bordeaux to Brussels

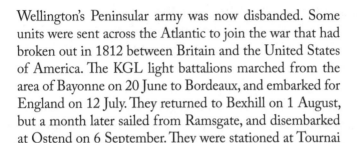

Wellington's Peninsular army was now disbanded. Some units were sent across the Atlantic to join the war that had broken out in 1812 between Britain and the United States of America. The KGL light battalions marched from the area of Bayonne on 20 June to Bordeaux, and embarked for England on 12 July. They returned to Bexhill on 1 August, but a month later sailed from Ramsgate, and disembarked at Ostend on 6 September. They were stationed at Tournai in Belgium, which now formed part of the United Netherlands under the Dutch King, William I.[19]

While returning from leave in Hanover, Lindau was attacked at Lemgo, twenty miles west of Hamelin, by some soldiers from the Principality of Lippe, and he stabbed one of them in the affray. Until the end of 1813, Lippe had belonged to Napoleon's grouping of German satellite states, the Confederation of the Rhine, and Lindau suspected that his attackers still had French sympathies.

Lindau also mentions the Beaulieu riflemen. They were, in fact, Hanoverian and were one of several units formed following the liberation of their country in 1813. Raised by Lieutenant-Colonel Karl von Beaulieu, they became known as the Grubenhagen Light Battalion and fought at Waterloo as part of a Hanoverian infantry brigade in the 3rd Division.

From Bayonne we marched to Bordeaux at the beginning of June and moved into a large camp there, where we had very many entertainments. Here we received our pay for the last nine months and we had the opportunity to dispose of our money; since many tents were put up with food and drink, tightrope walkers and circus riders had also appeared; the peasants from the vicinity had produced whole rows of casks of wine. We only had to exercise a little, we could recover from the exertions of the Spanish campaign and take pleasure in the life in England to which, so they said, we would be taken.

In the summer of the year 1814 our 2nd Battalion was embarked on a three-decker, the biggest ship in the English fleet, we were told. The admiral had a room as big as a hall and as fine as I had only seen in Madrid and San Sebastian; on either side of the ship were three tiers of cannon, and three hundred sailors and three hundred marines served on it. On this ship were cows, pigs, geese and hens. The sailors were under strict discipline; I have often seen how a sailor who was last out of the room when the pipe sounded would be administered some of the rope's end by the boatswain. In fine weather they had to climb the ropes up above for practice, which we were often allowed to watch for a whole hour. For the most part, though, we had to remain in our berths below since on the deck we would be in the way of the sailors in their work.

Soon after landing in England we were again embarked for the Netherlands, where I only stayed eight days with the battalion; then all who lived on the far side of the Rhine could get discharge or leave. I and Corporal Weissleder took leave, we had to hand in our rifles and our cartridge cases and travel with our bayonets at our side to our homeland. On the second day we encountered a Jew, who marched with us for some days. To begin with he was very cautious but on the third day, when he had gained confidence in us, he said that he had three hundred thalers on him and since we had been such good fellow travellers to him he wanted to serve us breakfast in his house, where we would soon be. He did indeed fetch us a big black pudding with a good glass of rum as well as paying for the journey, which we resumed again to a boat.

We then came into a town where, when the name of the commandant was mentioned to us, my corporal grew pale and said, 'Now I am lost. He was my major when I was in the Dutch service; I deserted and the man will know me again.' Nevertheless, I allayed his fears, took both passes, said that I was Corporal Weissleder and let the pass be examined. My friend waited for me in the meantime with fear in his heart and then we moved on as quickly as possible. In Holland we one day paid for a wagon and in the next village abandoned it in front of the house of the burgomaster. Here Weissleder produced a letter* that stated that we were to pick up recruits from Hanover, for which the burgomaster gave us a wagon. So we let ourselves be supplied with a wagon as far as Osnabrück; but then we dared not make any further use of our letter.

After some days I came to my home town after dark. I walked into my parents' house, and announced myself in a rough voice as a good friend of their son bringing greetings from him. My mother at once got up and embraced me, there was great joy in the house, the neighbours came in to see me, showed me great respect and demanded that I tell my story endlessly, which became rather tiresome for

---

* A forged requisition.

me. My father listened to me very closely; he himself had been a Hanoverian soldier for twenty-three years but they had not done such deeds, he thought. Then he told me how he and some other fathers several years before had been summoned to the town hall, where they were ordered to produce their children. 'Mine', he had said, 'are in the English service; I would gladly have them here but the English would not surrender them to me; perhaps the commissioner would have the goodness to send some policemen after them.' Then he was chased out by the French commanders.

After fourteen days I took leave of my parents, hoping that we should soon see each another again. In Pyrmont I met Corporal Weissleder again and marched with him to Lemgo. Here I visited my old master, the son of leather worker Müller, and the friend with whom I had earlier stayed a night in secret. At about eight o'clock in the evening I went with Müller into Jakobsen's tavern, where we drank a glass of rum. In the bar there were some Lippe soldiers who talked to one another, but in a language I could not understand. My friend Müller at once asked me to leave with him because the soldiers, who still served with the French in their hearts, wanted to take my life.

When we came out on to the street it was already very dark; we supported one another and hurried out. I immediately received a blow on my neck from behind with a stick, my hat fell off my head and Müller ran away. When I had put my hat on again two people came at me with drawn sabres. I struck the sword out of the hand of the first and I ran through the second with my bayonet so that he cried out loudly and fell down. I wiped off my blade, put it in its sheath and went into my lodging.

I had scarcely got there when the guard appeared and asked which of us two had stabbed the man. 'I did it,' was my answer; someone demanded my blade, and I refused to hand it over. The corporal of the guard stepped forward and threatened to knock me down at once if I did not obey. I for my part threatened him if he did not let me alone. 'I will go to the guardhouse,' I then said to him, 'but I will keep my bayonet since I will not let myself be ill treated by you; I will cut anyone who comes near me to pieces.' Then Weissleder stepped forward, slung on his bayonet and said: 'I will bring him to the guardhouse, but first, anyone who wrongly seizes us is a dead man.' We then went to the guardhouse; the Lippe corporal and his people followed us. There I gave my bayonet to the sergeant and had to stay for the night.

The next morning I was led before the commandant, who told me that the drummer whom I had stabbed the day before would probably die and that then I must die too. I replied that I was not afraid; I had been attacked with a murderous weapon and therefore I would stand under English protection; it was by no means acceptable to pass sentence here. The commandant rebuked me for what I had said, called the corporal and let me be taken to the guardhouse again. But the next morning at nine o'clock I was dragged out again; six men and a corporal stood there and loaded their muskets before my eyes. Then the adjutant said that I would see that the six men had loaded, if I looked about to run away, the six bullets would be sent after me. I replied that I did not think much of six bullets, many had already whistled past my ears. He told me to be quiet.

On the same day when it was dark, we came to Hamelin and I was brought before Commander von Bülow, who was surprised to see me again so soon. After I had told him the story and he had written a little on the corporal's paper he said to him: 'Go away, hand over the paper and greet your Princess,'* and turning to me he said, in the corporal's presence, 'You will find a lodging at Hupe the shoemaker.' I asked to be allowed to stay in the guardhouse and to be sent away as soon as possible so that my parents would not come to know about this. He granted my request and after two days I was sent to Hanover with two NCOs from the Hamelin Battalions, Pertz and Schlemm.

After I had spent eight days there at the Clever-Thor, where I received my rations regularly, I marched with a transport of fifty arms wagons and a hundred and fifty men to Brabant under the command of Major von Struve. It was late in the year by now and the snow already lay one foot deep. However I was a prisoner so I did not want to be with the militia, who wore red coats, but kept myself with a small detachment of Beaulieu riflemen, who were glad to have me with them and let me tell them all about myself. Instead of the fifty wagons with the Dutchmen, we had two hundred and fifty essential carriages, which were badly needed. Shortly before Antwerp we lost some of the carriages, and I was sent after them with a Beaulieu rifleman while the main transport moved on. Two hours later we arrived in Antwerp, where Major Struve rode

* The Prince of Lippe, Leopold II, was a minor and his mother, Princess Pauline, acted as regent. Whether the soldiers were actually to report to her or whether they were simply told to go home is an open question.

towards us anxiously and ordered me to report at the chief guardhouse. No one asked after me for many days and I received no rations, although I requested them many times from the sergeant on guard duty. I did not go short, though, partly because I had money and partly because I was allowed to eat with the comrades from the militia, for whom I constantly had to retell my story.

At last I learnt that there was a corporal from our battalion in Antwerp; I reported to him and on the next day I was sent to Brussels with a transport. Just before the gate of the city Adjutant Riefkugel, who was going for a ride, came to meet us; he asked me why I had been so long. 'On leave,' was my answer, 'but I wish that I had not seen Germany since things turned out badly for me there.'

'We know that already,' he said, 'tomorrow morning you will be hanged!'

'The rope will not be made by then!' I replied. He rode away laughing. I had been in the guardhouse for an hour and it was two o'clock in the afternoon, parade was just mounted, and then I was brought to Colonel Halkett. Our regimental paymaster was in the anteroom, and I had to tell him of my adventure in Germany, for which he paid me a thaler. When I was marched in to Colonel Halkett he interrogated me carefully and then said: 'I hope that nothing like this happens to me again – we know what you are like. Here is a thaler for you, but you are not to go out of the barracks tonight.' My company received me back with joy; Corporal Weissleder was particularly glad to see me again; a 'welcome' was drunk to me and I did not go out on the binge; wine was fetched, and more than the two thalers that had been given me were gone by the next day.

7

THE WATERLOO CAMPAIGN
1815

After his fall, Napoleon had been exiled to the Mediterranean island of Elba, but he now escaped and landed with a small escort on the southern coast of France on 1 March 1815. Nineteen days later, he reached Paris and regained power, having won over the troops sent by King Louis XVIII to stop him.

Once again, the European powers mobilised to invade France. To pre-empt them, Napoleon decided to take the offensive and seize Belgium, where two Allied armies were assembling: a Prussian force under Field Marshal Gebhard von Blücher, and an Anglo-Dutch-German composite army under Wellington.

Wellington complained that he had 'an infamous army'. Overall, it was inferior to the magnificent machine that had been broken up at the end of the Peninsular War, but it did contain some experienced units and commanders, and veterans like Lindau. Napoleon's own army was seriously flawed because of its hurried organisation: the reduced quality of some of its formations, notably the Imperial Guard, and its distrust of many of its generals following the recent political upheavals.

Nearly all the KGL was with Wellington in Belgium, including all five of the cavalry regiments, and eight of the ten infantry battalions. But it did not fight as a corps, for Wellington dispersed its regiments and brigades throughout his army to stiffen his more unsteady contingents. The two light battalions were brigaded with the 5th and 8th Line Battalions under Colonel Christian von Ompteda.* In the typically careful way that Wellington built his army, Ompteda's reliable brigade was combined with two less-experienced ones, one British and the other Hanoverian, to form the 3rd Division.

The KGL was weaker than before, for most of its non-Hanoverian men had been discharged or transferred to other corps after the end of the Peninsular War. Furthermore, its battalions were reduced in April 1815 from ten to six companies each, in order to release cadres of officers and NCOs to strengthen the *Landwehr* (militia) units of the new Hanoverian army.

Napoleon invaded Belgium on 15 June, striking between the two Allied armies in the hope of defeating them before they could concentrate and unite. The next day, Wellington contained the French left wing at the crossroads of Quatre-Bras, twenty miles south of Brussels, but Blücher was defeated six miles further south-east at Ligny and retreated northwards.

Ompteda's brigade was not present at Quatre-Bras, having been left nine miles to the west in case Napoleon tried to outflank Wellington by directing another invasion thrust through Mons. But Lindau saw the battlefield the next day, the 17th, and records his horror at the carnage.

Wellington then retreated to a new and stronger position, a ridge 2.5 miles south of the town of Waterloo.

---

* Formerly Major Christian von Ompteda.

There, he gave battle on the 18th after receiving assurances that Blücher would march to his support. Ompteda's brigade was placed at the centre of the line, and the 2nd Light Battalion was detached to hold the farmstead of La Haye Sainte, 250 yards in front of the ridge crest, as an advanced strongpoint.

'WE WERE SOON UP TO OUR KNEES IN WATER'

In this winter of 1814–15 and in the spring of 1815 we were in more towns and had a good lifestyle, for we received over sixteen Mariengroschen pay each day. This lasted until the middle of June. On 16 June at midday we received the order to hold ourselves ready to march straight away. About evening we heard in the far distance the rumble of cannon and we were surprised because we had not yet heard anything from the enemy nearby. As darkness came we broke camp and marched all night long. In the half-light of the morning a camp follower from Hamelin came to us; she was called Ehlers Wieschen and had married a husband by the name of Pieper. She asked after her husband; I could not say where he was, but I persuaded her to give me a measure of rum in my canteen, which she stubbornly refused to accept payment for out of friendliness to a fellow countryman.

At daybreak we were posted in a sunken road, from where we soon marched left and came to the battlefield where the Brunswickers had suffered so badly the previous day. It was a horrible field of corpses and was literally swimming in blood, which at every step went over our ankles. Then we marched around a wood where the enemy was meant to be and spread out as skirmishers, but the order came for us to draw back. After half an hour – it might well have been four o'clock – it suddenly became dark as night; lightning flashes lit up the darkness and the crash of thunder accompanied the roar of the cannon. We pressed so closely together that we could all have fitted into a large room and let the rain pour down on us. The downpour was so violent that we were soon standing up to our knees in water.

When the terrible rain lessened somewhat we marched along a highway on which our cavalry passed us in its advance against the enemy. In the space of an hour our riders pressed forward three times and three times came back again. They were so completely muddy that we could no longer recognise the colour of their uniforms and were sometimes unsure whether they were friend or enemy. Towards evening we marched through a high cornfield that we turned to mud under our feet so that it looked as though it had been reaped after us; and then we reached the farm La Haye Sainte, which lay close to the road.

Two companies were immediately sent into the vegetable garden, which did not at all please me as I could not find any dry spot. Therefore I went to look for some straw in the farm behind, where I found my brother, who could not let me have anything as nothing more was to be found in the barn. Just then Major Baring came out of the house and commanded that the livestock in the stalls should be slaughtered; the meat was shared with the people from the line battalion stationed outside, who had come to get straw. Meanwhile I had discovered some peas on the floor of the house and taken a pocketful; I hurried back into the garden with these and a large piece of meat to my comrades, whom I asked to light a fire. But since it continued to rain non-stop and the garden was deep in mud no one was willing to do so; some stood leaning against a tree or a wall, others had sat on their packs and stared straight ahead. None of them wanted to lie down.

So I went back into the farm, heard that there was wine in the cellar, crept in, found a half-full barrel and filled my canteen. Carrying this, I looked for my youngest brother, who had told me that he was posted with his battery in our proximity. It was he whom I had forcibly driven back home from Rohrsen seven years before; we had not seen each other since then. In front of the barn door I found people from our 1st Battalion who almost drained my canteen; then I went out into the dark again and soon was challenged by a patrol. I knew the corporal who led the patrol: my fellow countryman Meyer, who served with the Bremen Field Battalion; the next day he was seriously wounded and fell into the hands of the French, and now lives in Hamelin as a pensioner and book deliveryman. I asked him about my brother but he could not give me any information. So I gave out my wine anyway and marched with the patrol to the farm, went once again into the cellar and brought back my canteen and that of Corporal Meyer full up. The patrol drank mine empty and Meyer took his with him; later on I went several more times into the cellar and provided my comrades in the garden with wine.

At midnight I had to take post at the end of the garden facing the enemy, then I sat on my pack and fell asleep. In the half-light of the morning my rear rank man woke me. He was called Harz and was born in Harze. He said, 'Stand up and give me a little wine; today is going to be a tough day and I am going to die because I dreamt quite definitely that I would get a bullet through my body that did me no misfortune and that I slept contented.'

'Dreams don't matter,' was my reply, 'come here, an abatis is being made, we will help, which will get us warm, since there is no more wine.' We pushed half a cart on to the road where the orchard was close to the building, others brought ladders and farm implements and three spiked French cannon were pushed there.

Battle of Waterloo

The 2nd Light Battalion was commanded by Major George Baring and contained about 380–400 men of all ranks. Of its six companies, two held the building block of La Haye Sainte, another the garden on the rear, or northern, side of the farm, and the remaining three the orchard on the southern side.

La Haye Sainte was a crucial stronghold, as it constricted the French attacks as they swept across the valley to assail the ridge crest further north. But if Napoleon managed to seize the farm, he would be able to use it as a forward base where he could assemble attacking units, bring up artillery, and wear down Wellington's centre at close range.

The first French assault on the farm came early in the afternoon, when Napoleon launched his main attack against Wellington's eastern wing. It was beaten off, but Baring suffered heavy losses. Lindau describes sallying

forth from the main gate of La Haye Sainte as two
brigades of British heavy cavalry overthrew the French
attacking formations on either side of the farm. (He
mistakenly describes the British horsemen as hussars.)

As the battle progressed a succession of reinforcements
was sent to La Haye Sainte: two companies of the
1st Light Battalion, the light company of the 5th Line
Battalion, and two hundred infantrymen from the German
state of Nassau. But Baring ran dangerously low on rifle
ammunition, and his pleas for more were to no avail. It
was impossible for Lindau's battalion to use musket
ammunition, because the bore of the rifle barrels was too
small: a Brown Bess musket had a calibre of 0.760 inches,
compared to just 0.615 inches for the Baker rifle. A cart of
rifle ammunition for Ompteda's brigade had overturned
in the confusion behind Wellington's army, and in any
case it would have been difficult, once the French attacks
began, to drive a cart down the barricaded main road to
the farm's main gate, or across the soaked fields to the barn
and farmyard gates on the western side of the building
block, since all these entrances were near the southern end
of the farm and exposed to French fire. Resupplying the
garrison through the windows and door of the northern
side of the farm would have required large quantities of
ammunition to be laboriously carried in by hand.

Nor had Baring been able to prepare the post properly
for defence. The great barn door on the western side of the
farm had been used as firewood, and the battalion's pioneers
had been sent to Wellington's other main strongpoint, the
farm of Hougoumont. Baring's men had made loopholes,
but had been unable to block the entrance to the barn
effectively. Lindau was helping to defend this entrance
when Baring noticed that he was bleeding badly from a
head wound and ordered him to withdraw. Lindau's refusal

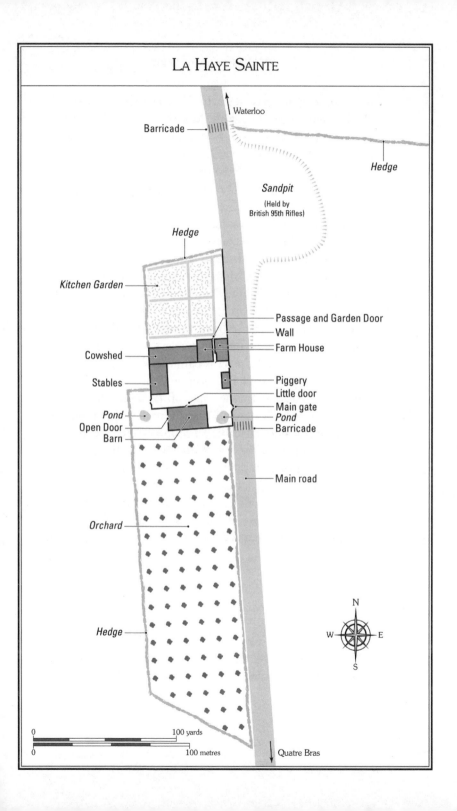

to do so, and his past record of bravery, resulted in him being awarded the Guelphic Medal, and he was singled out for special mention in both North Ludlow Beamish's *History of the King's German Legion* and William Siborne's classic *History of the Waterloo Campaign.*[20]

Towards 18.00, a final French attack began to overwhelm the defence, and Baring reluctantly had to order his surviving men to abandon the farm. Just over half the garrison made it back to Wellington's main position. Many accounts of the battle suggest that there were just forty-two survivors, but this is, in fact, false. Major Baring reported that he had just forty-two men of the 2nd Light Battalion left with him at the end of the battle, but others had dispersed after escaping from the farm in order to search for ammunition. Nor did Baring's figure of forty-two include men from the other units that had helped his battalion defend the farm.

In 1998, the Bexhill Hanoverian Study Group added a memorial plaque to the wall of La Haye Sainte to commemorate both the 2nd Light Battalion and Colonel von Ompteda, who fell leading a counter-attack by the 5th Line Battalion after the fall of the farm. On the opposite side of the road stands the Hanoverian monument, erected in 1818 on the site of a mass grave and inscribed with the names of the fallen officers of the KGL. As many as 63 per cent of the officers of Lindau's battalion were killed, wounded or captured at Waterloo.

First, about midday, the thunder of the French cannon rolled over towards us; we stood ready to fire behind the hedge and waited for the enemy. It was not long before a swarm of enemy skirmishers came, a thousand rifles exploded and a jubilant cry '*en avant!*'* resounded; behind them were two columns of enemy troops of the line who marched forwards so quickly that we said to one another: 'The French are in such a hurry, it's as if they wanted to eat in Brussels today.' At first, as the enemy were packed in front of our hedge we opened such murderous fire on the dense crowd that the ground was immediately covered with a mass of wounded and dead. For a moment the French halted, then they fired, causing major destruction on us. My friend Harz collapsed at my side with a bullet through his body, Captain Sch̄au̅ nn from the 2nd Battalion fell too, my brother too̅ n on his back and carried him into the farm, where ̄aid him down, but he was already dead. We did n̄t w ̄ ̄w from our position, but when the columns on ̄ ̄ ̄ advanced as far as the barn door and threatened t̄ ̄ut off our withdrawal into its entrance, we marched slowly back, shooting. Major Bösewiel was wounded during this: I saw him lying on the ground, he stood up once more then fell on his face and died.

Now the enemy stood at the entrance to the barn, we drove them back and went inside, admittedly with many casualties. Then we gave such unbroken fire in the barn behind – towards the open entrance – in front of which the French were thickly massed, that they did not attempt to enter. I stood here for perhaps half an hour, then, as the pressure of the French became weaker I moved in front of a loophole near the closed gate that led to the highway. The French stood so closely packed here that several times I saw three or four enemy fall by one bullet. A short time

---

* 'Forward.'

after that Captain Graeme* opened the wing of the gate and we attacked the close-standing enemy with fixed bayonets. They did not hold their position as we pressed forward with overpowering boldness. I stabbed and cut blindly into the crowd. We followed the enemy over the abatis, when suddenly English hussars appeared at our side, hacking into the enemy so furiously that a great crowd of them turned back to us without their weapons and asked for quarter. The hussars had meanwhile come back from their pursuit and led the prisoners away with them.

Behind the abatis we now awaited a new assault; it was barely half an hour in coming. We held the skirmishers back with little trouble, but when the fresh columns stormed up we moved into the gateway, which I barred on Captain Graeme's orders. I took up position with some others in front of the loophole near the gateway, through which we shot at the enemy where they were densest, then quickly stepped back to load and make room for the others. Of course the French also put their muskets in the opening and more of my comrades fell near me; some also came falling down from the stand above, from which our people were shooting over the wall. But that only increased our determination, so I could hardly wait until I fired another round and I loaded my rifle with such eagerness that I shot over a hundred rounds that day.

New regiments were continually brought up but regularly beaten back. An enemy officer fell to me nearby; he had been constantly riding round the battlefield in front of us and showing the way to the advancing columns. For

---

* Properly Lieutenant Graeme. Company commanders like Graeme and Ole Lindam were generally called 'captain', even if their rank was lieutenant.

some time I had him in my sights – at last, just as he was leading up new troops, he came into my fire. His horse made a bound, reared up and fell with the rider beneath it. Soon afterwards we made a sally. I opened the gateway, the nearest enemy were bayoneted and the others fled. We hurried behind them for a distance and halted.

Now I saw not far from me the officer whom I had shot; I rushed up to him and took hold of his gold watch chain; I had scarcely got it in my hand than he raised his sabre by way of reprimand, I gave him a blow on the forehead with my rifle butt so that he fell back and dropped dead, when I noticed a gold ring on his finger. I first cut the little bag from his horse and was just about to take the ring off him when my comrades called out, 'Get a move on and come away, the cavalry are making a fresh charge.' I saw some thirty riders spring forward and I ran very quickly with my booty to my comrades, who forced the enemy to withdraw with a salvo.

We halted then for a while on the highway and I was glad to see heaps of dead enemy lying more then a foot high near the abatis. By the wall I saw a grenadier lying with a bullet through his body; he wanted to run himself through the breast with a sabre, but no longer had the necessary strength to do it. I seized the hilt of the sword to throw it away; the Frenchman let go immediately, no doubt fearing that I might wound his hands by pulling it away. Near the abatis a wounded man with a bullet through the leg lay in a pool of water; he cried out loudly in pain and tried to roll out of the water. I seized him by the arms and another took hold of his legs and so we laid him by the wall with his head on a comrade who had been shot.

Running around near us were some wounded English horses, some twenty to thirty at most; I called out to one of them, it stood still and let me lead it into the farm, where I brought it to Major Baring. He ordered me to chase it out of the farm immediately. Then I showed him a purse with gold coins, a booty that I had found a short while before. I asked him to look after it for me. But he refused to accept it, saying 'Who knows what lies before us today? You must look after the money the best way yourself.'

Soon after this the farm was stormed again and my captain ordered me to remain by the gateway. This time the battle lasted longer as ever more columns advanced; We soon ran short of cartridges, so that as soon as one of our men fell we immediately went through his pockets. At the same time Major Baring, who constantly rode round the farm, reassured us that fresh ammunition would soon arrive. Soon afterwards I got a bullet through the back of my head,* which I informed my captain about as he stood above me on the platform. He ordered me to go back. 'No,' I answered, 'so long as I can stand I stay at my post.'

Meanwhile I undid my scarf, wet it with rum and asked one of my comrades to pour rum into the wound and tie the scarf round my head. I attached my hat firmly to my pack and reloaded my rifle. My captain above me, whom I could see every time I loaded, turned to order and rebuke me repeatedly across the wall as he fell upon the French. I warned him not to put himself so far over the wall since he could easily be shot. 'That doesn't matter,' was his reply, 'let the dogs fire.' But immediately afterwards I saw how

---

* This was a severe head wound noted on Lindau's discharge papers.

his hand was bleeding and how he had tied a handkerchief around it. Then I cried out, 'Now, captain, you can go back.' 'Nonsense,' he replied, 'no going back; that won't do.' He took his sword in his left hand and went forward to attack the enemy that were streaming out.

Soon after that I heard a cry at the door of the barn: 'The enemy mean to get through here.' I went there and had scarcely fired a few shots down into the barn when I noticed thick smoke under the beam. Major Baring and Sergeant Reese from Tündern and Poppe immediately hurried in with kettles that they had filled at a pond to empty in the barn. The loopholes behind us were now weakly manned and the French maintained heavy fire on us through them, but it became weaker and I and some of my comrades went back in front of the loopholes.

Then just as I had fired, a Frenchman seized my rifle to snatch it away. I said to my neighbour, 'Look, the dog has seized my rifle.'

'Wait,' he said, 'I have a bullet,' and at once the Frenchman fell. At the same moment another seized my rifle, but my next man on the right stabbed him in the face. I needed to draw my rifle back to load it, but a mass of bullets flew by me, rattling on the stone of the wall. One took the worsted tuft from my shoulder. Another shattered the cock on my rifle.

In order to get another rifle I hurried by the pond where the above-mentioned Reese lay dying. He could no longer speak. But when I went to take his rifle (I knew it was very good) he pulled an angry face. I looked for another – there were plenty around – and took my place again at my loophole. I had soon fired my shots, though, and before I could shoot again I had to search the pockets of my fallen comrades for ammunition, but they were mostly empty by now. Thus our fire became weaker and the pressure of the French grew. Our barn again caught fire; the fire was again put out. I made a thorough search of the cartridge pouches of the fallen in the farm. Then Major Baring rode up to me and said, 'You must go back.' But I replied to him, as I had already answered Captain Graeme, 'It would be a cur who left you while his head is on his shoulders.'

THE END OF THE BATTLE

Lindau was captured when La Haye Sainte finally fell. But Napoleon failed to break through Wellington's position on the ridge further north, and in the evening, after a final, vain attack by the Imperial Guard, the French army dissolved into flight. By that stage, Lindau was being taken to the rear by his captors, and found himself caught up in the rout.

But soon afterwards I heard a general shouting throughout the farm, 'Defend yourselves, defend yourselves! They are coming over everywhere. Come together.' Our people had left the stand; I saw more Frenchmen on the wall. One of them jumped down on the stand but in that instant I ran him through the chest with a bayonet. He collapsed on me and I flung him to one side, but my bayonet was bent, so I had to detach it. At the entry to the farmhouse I saw my captain fighting hand to hand with the French. One of them was about to shoot Ensign Frank but Captain Graeme stabbed him with a sword through his body, another he struck in the face.

I wanted to rush to help, but then I found myself suddenly surrounded by the French. Now I used the butt of my rifle and hit out in all directions around me so that I soon had only the barrel of my weapon in my hands and disengaged again. I heard swearing and invective behind me: '*Couyons Hanovriens*' and '*Anglais*', and saw two Frenchmen bringing Captain Holtzermann into the barn. I wanted to free him, but suddenly a Frenchman at my side grabbed the front of my clothes, I pounced on him too. Another stabbed at me with his bayonet, but I threw the Frenchman whom I had grabbed round to the side so that he received the thrust; he let go of me and with the cry, '*Mon Dieu, mon Dieu!*' fell down.

I now hurried towards the barn, hoping to escape that way; I found the exit strongly manned so I jumped over the lower shearing where some of my comrades were standing with Captain Holtzermann. Soon many French came to us and cried '*En avant, couyons!*' We were forced out of the corner in which we were standing and compelled to jump over the shearing, whereby one of us, for whom the jump was difficult because of a wound, got a blade through his loins. That stirred us up: we cursed the French and wanted to attack them, but Captain Holtzermann managed to pacify our anger in spite of our seething over this disgraceful treatment, the kind of which a single French prisoner had never experienced from us.

We were taken out of the barn, across the farmyard, through the gateway and on to the highway, where many French crowded round us, seized hold of us and plundered us. One of them snatched away my breadbag and found in it the purse of gold coins, whereupon another grabbed at it at once but the first held it fast and a violent quarrel instantly developed. Next my knapsack was torn from my shoulders. Others pulled at my equipment, feeling for the watches, and finding them – I had one gold and two silver watches. When they had taken everything from me I became angry and punched a Frenchman, who still hoped to find something on me, in the face. Then two cannon-shot from our side fell, striking down a crowd of Frenchmen and taking away some of ours. The enemy hesitated for a moment and then tore Captain Holtzermann's sash and scabbard from him. We grabbed stones and wanted to avenge such offensive behaviour on the part of hated French, but our captain calmed us down and turned to a French officer whom we recognised as one we had held prisoner at the Jewish cemetery by Bayonne. He tried to protect us and forbade his people to rob but was laughed at and rebuked.

We still hoped that the English riders would make an advance; we would then at once make an attack on the enemy. But French cuirassiers appeared, almost all with bound-up heads, and led us further along the road. They forced us to run as fast as their horses and stabbed a man from the 1st Battalion dead through the loins because he could not run fast enough. For an hour we were held between the French infantry, which stood in line to the right and left of us, as the French army in broken order – artillery, cavalry and infantry in confusion – came behind us. As for ourselves, even in our sad situation we felt an indescribable joy and communicated it by exchanging glad looks with shining eyes; I whispered to my neighbour, 'Were we now a hundred armed men we could take the whole army prisoner.' After about three hours it was evening and we were taken into a completely dark barn, where we met other prisoners. Scarcely were we in there than French infantry, fleeing troops with no discipline or order, burst open the door and began to rob us. In this confusion I pushed myself outside with some comrades. It was moonlight and I noticed how everywhere was swarming with fleeing French.

I had been tormented by a raging thirst for a long time, so I hurried, regardless of my safety, to a well that I had noticed nearby. Here I found some French guards and asked one, in French, for water. 'You are no Frenchman,' he said in German. 'What country are you from?'

'I am a Hanoverian.'

'And where from there?'

'I am from Hamelin on the Weser.'

'I was in that town', he continued, 'when the general sold us.'

'Why are you now with the French?' I asked.

'Because I could not stand captivity,' he answered, 'I took service.' Then he gave me a jar full of water and a piece of bread. Next Corporal Fastermann came by; he had also escaped from the barn and was given a drink and a piece of bread. The guardsman advised us to keep to the right, where the Prussians were; on the left was the French army in retreat. 'In one hour', he added, 'we shall all be in the hands of the English.'

I thanked the man, shook his hand and hurried to the right with Corporal Fastermann and thus we came unharmed into a young wood, where we sat down in a small hollow, since I was very tired. It must have been about midnight and was very cold. My limbs trembled and my teeth chattered. To the right of us all was quiet, but on the left we could hear the French shooting sporadically and continually calling out, '*Vive l'Empereur!*' The cold drove us on after half an hour, and cautiously we continued our march through the wood. We soon came to the end of it and went for a stretch over open country where all was still and we could only hear the noise of the surviving French on the retreat in the distance.

AFTERMATH

After escaping, Lindau was sent to Brussels to recover from his wounds, before rejoining his battalion at Paris. He was discharged on 24 October. The KGL itself was disbanded the following year, and its men were incorporated into the Hanoverian army. During its thirteen-year existence, it had served as far afield as Germany, Ireland, Sweden, Denmark, Portugal, Spain, Gibraltar, Italy, Sicily, Malta, Belgium and France. Twenty-eight thousand NCOs and men enlisted in the KGL at some point during its existence. As many as one in five of them died, either in battle, at sea, from disease or from other causes.[21] Nevertheless the KGL came to be counted as amongst Wellington's best troops.

Then we came to a defile and for greater safety went into it; but immediately we heard a noise in front of us and the cry: '*Halt la, qui vit?*'*

'Friend!' answered Fastermann. He fixed a bayonet.

'Fastermann, protect yourself!' I said, but he charged against the Frenchman, seized him by the throat and pushed him against the side of the defile. I tried to seize his rifle, but in vain; then I took the bayonet off and gave the Frenchman two stabs in his body. Fastermann now took the rifle and so we were both armed, to some extent. We listened and lay with our ears on the ground, but everything was quiet, so we went further in the defile.

On the way out of this we found a large barn with the door partly open. I crept cautiously in, heard French curses and immediately turned back to my comrade. What should we do now? It was already the half-light of the morning but a thick mist surrounded us and we had lost our way. We decided to hide in a small stable that was near and where no one, we hoped, would look for us. But we had only been in it a few minutes when close above our heads we heard a rustling and banging and a high-pitched cry. We sank down in fear and my knees shook. The next moment we laughed at ourselves: a cock had greeted the new morning and we found we were in a hen house.

The lodging did not suit us; we hurried further on and were scarcely into open country when a peasant ran past us. Fastermann ordered him to stop, but the peasant did not listen. Fastermann threatened him with a shot, he stood still then and told us that he wanted to fetch the Prussians,

---

* 'Halt! Who goes there?'

who had halted about a quarter of an hour from there on a knoll, for the French were plundering his village and wanted to set it on fire. We hurried away with the peasant and soon came on a Prussian outpost of two lancers; we were challenged, they asked where we came from and who we were. An officer soon came up with a squadron alongside, he learned from the peasant the situation in his village and galloped away; the peasant hurried after him.

One of the lancers then brought us into a neighbouring village,* which was quite full of Prussians; the Prussians were looking in the dirt for valuables on the street that ran through the village, since Napoleon's carriage had been plundered here during the night. In the doorway of the neighbouring house we were shown this carriage. The doors stood open, it was lined with velvet, a sofa was in it and behind that was a kitchenette. We were then led into a house, given bread and meat and shown a cellar where we could get wine. We went in with a bucket and we found water in the cellar a foot high, so that we had to scoop it out standing on the stairs. As we lay down to rest we first realised that we were tired to death, moreover the wound in my head was causing me great pain. A doctor was called and washed the congealed blood from my head and neck and covered the wound with an adhesive plaster.

After some hours we were taken some way further on a wagon, as far as an inn that our troops would pass; here we lay in the ditch by the street and waited. Some individual Dutch came by, but they could give us no information; finally an officer showed us the direction in

---

* Genappe.

which we had to go to find our people. We set out again and with heartfelt joy soon saw our own people, but in what formation? There were altogether perhaps only one hundred men. I went up to Major Baring and greeted him; he enquired after our lot and asked how many of us had escaped. For half an hour I marched further with the battalion, until it camped; then Adjutant Riefkugel came and brought me the order that I should return to Brussels. I refused and said that nothing was wrong with me and expressed the wish not to be taken to the hospital. I turned to the major three times with my request, but always to no avail. By this time a wagon had been provided; I was not willing to get in but the adjutant ordered me and I had to obey. 'When you are healed then come back to us.' With this parting I set off on the road to Brussels.

Up till now I had suppressed my pain; but now I was alone and sad, the heat of the day was unbearable, I could not sleep and wished for death. Suddenly there was a cry of 'Halt!'; a Belgian major by the name of Twent, who had served in Spain with our battalion and who now was riding at the head of his battalion, came to me and asked, 'Aren't you Lindau?' I had to tell him how things had turned out for me. Then he gave me some wine from his canteen, drew a piece of white bread and a five-franc piece out of his pocket, gave me his hand and said that I was not to forget him. I have never been able to recall without emotion this kind behaviour that did me so much good in my lonely agony. On arrival in Brussels I was quartered in a citizen's house because the hospitals were full, and I was treated in a very friendly way by my hosts, but at the beginning especially I was in a great deal of pain and was always bored. It was only for the last week that I had the pleasure of living in a house with Captain Graeme.

After about four weeks I obtained permission from the doctor to go to my battalion and marched off to Paris with a detachment of three hundred men. Here first I met my brother*, who was standing with my company and who stared when he caught sight of me. 'Where have you come from, Friedrich?' he said to me, 'I thought you were dead, I looked for you on the battlefield, and found you and buried you.'

'Nonsense,' I said, 'who knows whom you have buried?' Some days later I met my other brother,† the artilleryman, who had also taken me for dead and had wanted to bury me in the battlefield. At that time I could not do any active service because of my wounds, so I was assigned to the depot where bread, corn, wood and straw were collected and thereby had a better life than my comrades in the camp. I liked service very much, but my head wound was very serious: I could not see properly and everything appeared larger than it really was and sometimes I could not really tell what I was doing. I asked for my discharge because of this condition; Major Baring refused it to me, since I would lose out by it, but I had set my mind on it and did not listen to sensible and well-intentioned advice. The major refused my wishes many times, but in the end when I did not weaken in my resolve I was given my discharge and marched into my homeland with the battery in which my youngest brother served.

---

* Georg Lindau.
† Christian Lindau.

APPENDICES

NARRATIVES OF THE PARTICIPATION OF THE 2ND LIGHT BATTALION OF THE KING'S GERMAN LEGION IN THE BATTLE OF WATERLOO

Appendix i

Major George Baring
Hanover, 12 March 1835

—————— ❧ ——————

The narrative was translated and published in English in Beamish's *History of the King's German Legion*, volume 2, page 453. This translation is accurate, but has some passages removed from the original German version. In this new translation of the original German account, provided by Gareth Glover, the text not printed by Beamish is shown in italics.[22]

—————— ❧ ——————

Preface of the Editor

In the days of Quatre-Bras and Waterloo, the Colonel and Brigade Commander George Baring acted as a major in the 2nd Light Battalion, the King's German Legion. In response to the request of the editorial staff he expressed his willingness that the following narrative, which he wrote a few weeks after the remarkable days as a private undertaking, be made available to the general public. It is written in a simple and unadorned language, which style is here maintained and the actions do not require any elaboration. The Colonel wished expressly that the reader be reminded that he writes in the first person. The editors preferred to keep the original form as any change in the wording would contradict the wishes of the Colonel.

*   *   *

The anticipation of the troops was very high, due to the return of Napoleon and the subsequent movements in France. The order of the day, 16 June 1815, instructed the battalions of the 3rd Division under the command of General Carl von Alten, to be moved from their quarters near Esscaussines and march to the village of Braine-le-Comte and at the same time move towards Nivelles.

The English and Hanoverian brigades marched to Quatre-Bras, while the 2nd German Legion moved under Colonel von Ompteda one hour away on the road to Mons and took position there. In the afternoon we heard a tremendous fire to our left without knowing its meaning. Before we knew the outcome, an order in the evening called us to join the division at Quatre-Bras, where we arrived at 12 midnight. At daylight, we saw the enemy opposite on the battlefield of the previous day.

A few shots marked the beginning of the new day, 17 June, otherwise both armies appeared to be inactive and we expected at any moment the order to attack. About 7 o'clock in the morning, I was called to General Alten and was told that the Prussian army to the left had been beaten the night before and consequently we were to fall back. At the same time I received an order to form a rearguard. I arranged that all forward positions would reduce their forces, formed a concentric position with the remainder and when the division had marched back far enough to lose visual contact with us, I started my own withdrawal.

Beside the battalion, I had under my command some Brunswick cavalry. Should the enemy breakout in force we would certainly lose in such open terrain, for which eventuality I was quite prepared.

Against all expectation, the enemy did not attack and I rejoined the division at Genappe, without firing a shot. After a short break, we started again at about 2 pm and at that moment the weather suddenly changed, there came on a tremendous storm with an unusually heavy rain and in a few minutes, the troops that were in the streets stood up to their knees in water. Everyone marched towards Brussels on the wide road and the troops were often stopped because of the congestion. It transpired that my Battalion and the 95th English Regiment were the last infantry.

The French attacked our men with power and had great success as they managed to throw our regiment over the hillock. I saw the enemy at a few hundred paces behind me and marched my battalion from the lanes into the fields to be ready to receive the enemy in a quarry. Colonel Barnard did the same with his 95th Regiment on the other side. We marched thus till half an hour before 8 [pm], to our position at Waterloo, without being attacked by the enemy's cavalry.

I was sent to the farm of La Haye Sainte in order to occupy it. We built defensive positions during the remainder of the daylight hours and as far as the rain allowed us and laid down in expectation of an attack the next morning.

The farm of La Haye Sainte lies, as is well known, close by the side of the high road which leads from Brussels to

Genappe, in the centre of the two positions, and about midway between them.

The dwelling-house, barn, and stables were surrounded by a rectangular wall, forming a court in the interior. Towards the enemy's side was an orchard, surrounded by a hedge, and in rear was a kitchen-garden, bounded by a small wall towards the road, but on the other sides by a hedge. Two doors and three large gates led from the court to the exterior; but of these, that of the barn had been unfortunately broken and burned by the troops.

The battalion consisted of six companies, which did not number 400 men; I posted three companies in the orchard, two in the buildings and one in the garden.

Important as the possession of this farm apparently was, the means of defending it were very insufficient, and besides, I was ordered, immediately on arriving there, to send off the pioneers of the battalion to Hougoumont, so that I had not even a hatchet; for unfortunately the mule that carried the entrenching tools was lost the day before.

As the day broke on 18 June, we sought out every possible means of putting the place in a state of defence, but the burned gate of the barn presented the greatest difficulty. With this employment, and cooking some veal which we found in the place, the morning was passed until after eleven o'clock, when the attack commenced against the left wing.

Every man now repaired to his post, and I betook myself to the orchard, where the first attack was to be expected; the farm lies in a hollow, so that a small elevation of the ground immediately in front of the orchard concealed the approach of the enemy.

Shortly after noon, some skirmishers commenced the attack. I made the men lie down and forbad all firing until the enemy were quite near. The first shot broke the bridle of my horse close to my hand, and the second killed Major Bösewiel, who was standing near me. The enemy did not stop long skirmishing, but immediately advanced over the height, with two close columns, one of which attacked the buildings, and the other threw itself in mass into the orchard, showing the greatest contempt for our fire. It was not possible for our small disjointed numbers fully to withstand this furious attack of such a superior force, and we retired upon the barn, in a more united position, in order to continue the defence: my horse's leg was broken, and I was obliged to take that of the adjutant.

Colonel von Klencke now came to our assistance with the Luneburg Battalion. We immediately recommenced the attack, and had already made the enemy give way, when I perceived a strong line of cuirassiers forming in front of the orchard; at the same time Captain Meyer came to me and reported that the enemy had surrounded the rear garden, and it was not possible to hold it longer. I gave him orders to fall back into the buildings, and assist in their defence. Convinced of the great danger which threatened us from the cuirassiers, in consequence of the weak hedge, so easy to break through, I called out to my men, who were mixed with the newly arrived Hanoverians – to assemble round me, as I intended retiring into the barn. The number of the battalion which had come to our assistance, exceeded, by many degrees, that of my men, and as at the same time, the enemy's infantry gained the garden – the skirmishers having been driven out by a column attack – the former, seeing the cuirassiers in the open field, imagined that their only chance of safety lay in gaining the main position of the army. My voice, unknown to them, and also not sufficiently penetrating, was, notwithstanding all my exertions, unequal to halt and collect my men together; already overtaken by the cavalry, we fell in with the enemy's infantry, who had surrounded the garden, and to whose fire the men were exposed in retiring to the main position. In this effort a part succeeded. Notwithstanding this misfortune, the farmhouse itself was still defended by Lieutenants George Graeme and Carey, and Ensign Frank. The English Dragoon Guards now came up – beat back the cuirassiers – fell upon the infantry, who had already suffered much, and nearly cut them to pieces.

In this first attack I lost a considerable number of men, besides three officers killed, and six wounded; on my requisition for support, Captains von Gilsa and Marschalck were sent to me, with their companies of the 1st Light Battalion; to these, and a part of my own battalion, I gave the defence of the garden, leaving the buildings to the three officers who had already so bravely defended them: the orchard I did not again occupy.

About half an hour's respite was now given us by the enemy, and we employed the time in preparing ourselves against a new attack; this followed in the same force as before; namely, from two sides by two close columns, which, with the greatest rapidity, nearly surrounded us, and, despising danger, fought with a degree of courage which I had never before witnessed in Frenchmen. Favoured by their advancing in masses, every bullet of ours hit, and seldom were the effects limited to one assailant; this did not, however, prevent them from throwing themselves against the walls, and endeavouring to wrest the arms from the hands of my men, through the loop-holes; many lives were sacrificed to the defence of the doors and gates; the most obstinate contest was carried on where the gate was wanting, and where the enemy seemed determined to enter. On this spot seventeen Frenchmen already lay dead, and their bodies served as a protection to those who pressed after them to the same spot.

Meantime four lines of French cavalry had formed on the right front of the farm; the first cuirassiers, second lancers, third dragoons, and fourth hussars, and it was clear to me that their intention was to attack the squares of our division in position, in order by destroying them to break the whole line. This was a critical moment, for what would be our fate if they succeeded! As they marched upon the position by the farm, I brought all the fire possible to bear upon them; many men and horses were overthrown, but they were not discouraged. Without in the least troubling themselves about our fire, they advanced with the greatest intrepidity, and attacked the infantry. All this I could see, and confess freely that now and then I felt some apprehension. The manner in which this cavalry was received and beaten back by our squares, is too well known to require mention here.

The contest in the farm had continued with undiminished violence, but nothing could shake the courage of our men, who, following the example of their officers, laughing, defied danger. Nothing could inspire more courage or confidence than such conduct. These are the moments when we learn how to feel what one soldier is to another – what the word 'comrade' really means – feelings which must penetrate the coarsest mind, but which he only can fully understand, who has been witness to such moments!

When the cavalry retired, the infantry gave up also their fruitless attack, and fell back, accompanied by our shouts, and derision. Our loss, on this occasion, was not so great as at first; however, my horse was again shot under me, and as my servant, believing me dead had gone away with my other horse, I procured one of those that were running about.

Our first care was to make good the injury which had been sustained; my greatest anxiety was respecting the ammunition, which, I found, in consequence of the continued fire, had been reduced more than one half. I immediately sent an officer back with this account, and requested ammunition, which was promised. About an hour had thus passed when I discovered the enemy's columns again advancing on the farm; I sent another officer back to the position with this intelligence, and repeated the request for ammunition.

Our small position was soon again attacked with the same fury, and defended with the same courage as before. Captain von Wurmb was sent to my assistance with the skirmishers of the 5th Line Battalion, and I placed them in the court; but welcome as this reinforcement was, it could not compensate for the want of ammunition, which every moment increased, so that after half an hour more of uninterrupted fighting, I sent off an officer with the same request.

This was as fruitless as the other two applications; however, two hundred Nassau troops were sent me. The principal contest was now carried on at the open entrance to the barn; at length the enemy, not being able to succeed by open force, resorted to the expedient of setting the place on fire, and soon a thick smoke was seen rising from the barn! Our alarm was now extreme, for although there was water in the court, all means of drawing it and carrying it were wanting – every vessel having been broken up. Luckily the Nassau troops carried large field cooking kettles; I tore a kettle from the back of one of the men; several officers followed my example, and filling the kettles with water, they carried them, facing almost certain death, to the fire. The men did the same and soon not one of the Nassauers was left with his kettle, and the fire was thus luckily extinguished – but alas, with the blood of many a brave man! Many of the men, although covered with wounds, could not be brought to retire. 'So long as our officers fight and we can stand,' was their constant reply, 'we will not stir from the spot.'

It would be injustice to a skirmisher named Frederick Lindau, if I did not mention him: bleeding from two wounds in the head and carrying in his pocket a considerable bag of gold which he had taken from an enemy officer, he stood at the small back barn door, and from thence defended the main entrance in his front. I told him to go back as the cloth about his head was not sufficient to stop the strong flow of blood; he however, as regardless of his wounds as of his gold, answered: 'He would be a scoundrel that deserted you, so long as his head is on his shoulders.' This brave fellow was afterwards taken, and lost his treasure.

This attack may have lasted about an hour and a half, when the French, tired from their fruitless efforts, again fell back. Our joy may well be imagined. With every next attack I became more convinced of the importance of holding the post. With every attack also, the weight of the responsibility that devolved upon me increased. This responsibility is never greater than when an officer is thus left to himself, and suddenly obliged to make a decision upon which perhaps, his own as well as the life and honour of those under him – nay even more important results – may depend. In battles, as is well known, trifles, apparently of little importance, have often incalculable influence.

What must have been my feelings, therefore, when, on counting the cartridges, I found that, on an average, there were not more than from three to four each! The men made nothing of the diminished physical strength which their excessive exertions had caused, and immediately filled up the holes that had been made in the walls by the enemy's guns, but they could not remain insensible to the position in which they were placed by the want of ammunition, and made the most reasonable remonstrances to me on the subject. These were not wanting to make me renew the most urgent representations, and finally to report specifically that I was not capable of sustaining another attack in the present condition. All was in vain! With what uneasiness did I now see two enemy columns again in march against us! At this moment I would have blessed the ball that came to deprive me of life. But more than life was at stake, and the extraordinary danger required extraordinary exertion and firmness. On my exhortations to courage and economy of the ammunition, I received one unanimous reply: 'No man will desert you, we will fight and die with you!' No pen, not even that of one who has experienced such moments, can describe the feeling which this excited in me; nothing can be compared with it! Never had I felt myself so elevated; but never also placed in so painful a position, where honour contended with a feeling for the safety of the men who had given me such an unbounded proof of their confidence.

The enemy gave me no time for thought; they were already close by our weak walls and now, irritated by the opposition which they had experienced, attacked with renewed fury. The contest commenced at the barn, which they again succeeded in setting on fire. It was extinguished, luckily, in the same manner as before. Every shot that was now fired increased my uneasiness and anxiety. I sent again to the rear with the positive statement that I must and would leave the place if no ammunition was sent me. This was also without effect.

Our fire gradually diminished, and in the same proportion did our perplexity increase; already I heard many voices calling out for ammunition, adding 'We will readily stand by you, but we must have the means of defending ourselves!' Even the officers, who, during the whole day, had shown the greatest courage, represented to me the impossibility of retaining the post under such circumstances. The enemy, who too soon observed our wants, now boldly broke in one of the doors; however, as only a few could come in at a time, these were instantly bayoneted, and the rear hesitated to follow. They now mounted the roof and walls, from which my unfortunate men were certain marks; at the same time they pressed in through the open barn, which could no longer be defended. Inexpressibly painful as the decision was of giving up the place, my feeling of duty as a man overcame that of honour, and I gave the order to retire through the house into the garden. How much these words cost me, and by what feelings they were accompanied, he only can judge who has been placed in a similar situation!

Fearing the bad impression which retiring from the house into the garden would make upon the men, and wishing to see whether it was possible still to hold any part of the place, I left to the before-mentioned three officers the honour of being the last. The passage through the house being very narrow, many of the men were overtaken by the enemy, who vented their fury upon them in the lowest abuse, and the most brutal treatment. Among the sufferers here was Ensign Frank, who had already been wounded: the first man that attacked him, he ran through with his sabre, but at the same moment, his arm was broken by a ball from another; nevertheless he reached a bedroom, and succeeded in concealing himself behind a bed. Two of the men also took refuge in the same place, but the French followed close at their heels, crying '*No pardon for you bastard greens!*', and shot them before his face: Frank had himself the good luck to remain undiscovered until the place again fell into our hands. As I was now fully convinced, and the officers agreed with me, that the garden was not to be maintained when the enemy were in possession of the dwelling house, I made the men retire singly to the main position. The French, pleased, perhaps, with their success, did not molest us in retreat. The men who had been sent to me from other regiments, I allowed to return, and with the weak remnant of my own battalion I attached myself to two companies of the 1st Light Battalion, which, under Lieutenant Colonel Lewis von dem Bussche, occupied the hollow road behind the farm. Although we could not fire a shot, we helped to increase the numbers. Here the combat recommenced with increased fury, the enemy pressing forth from the farm, and I had the pain to see Captain Henry von Marschalck fall – a friend whose distinguished coolness and bravery on this day I can never forget; Captain von Gilsa also had his right arm shattered; Lieutenant Albert was shot, and Lieutenant Graeme, as he swung his cap in the air to cheer on the men, had his right hand shattered; neither would go into the hollow road, not withstanding all my persuasions, but remained above upon the edge. On the retreat from the buildings Captain Holtzerman and Lieutenant Tobin were taken, and Lieutenant Carey was wounded, so that the number of my officers was very much reduced. I rode a Dragoon horse, in front of whose saddle were large pistol holsters and a cloak, and the firing was so sharp that four balls entered here, and another the saddle, just as I had alighted to replace my hat which had been knocked off by a sixth ball.

The 5th Line Battalion which stood on our right, were now ordered to attack the enemy with the bayonet. *The battalion made it with the greatest courage. In the moment when a certain disorder was inevitable, a regiment of cuirassiers came from the rear and gained terrible revenge for the decimation that their comrades had just suffered.*

The cuirassiers thought this a good opportunity to break through the line, not, perhaps, being aware of the presence of our men in the hollow road; however when they had arrived within about twenty paces, they received such a fire that they wheeled about in the greatest disorder, well marked by our men; at this moment the 3rd Hussars advanced.

The cuirassiers reformed with unbelievable speed and faced again. Both corps appeared not to trust each other, however they enticed the hussars in and the encounter about 200 paces from us was short but very bloody. After about a quarter of an hour of intense fighting both sides withdrew; the hussars were mixed amongst our infantry.

A strange incident took place here. A corporal from the hussars was surrounded by the cuirassiers, he managed to find a way between them; one cuirassier had the same fate between the hussars. Both wanted to rejoin their corps and met about half way, although the hussar was bleeding a lot, they attacked each other. All this was happening in full view of their respective comrades, nobody went forward to stop the fight. I feared for the hussar as I saw him bleeding; however, all his training showed above the strength of his opponent, and managed to get on his left side, gave a mighty blow to his face which laid him on the ground and he then rode calmly back to his side while his comrades were cheering and congratulating him.

Fresh columns of the enemy again advanced, and nothing seemed likely to terminate the slaughter but the entire destruction of one army or the other. My horse, the third which I had had in the course of the day, received a ball in his head; he sprung up, and in coming down again, fell on my right leg, and pressed me so hard into the deep loamy soil, that, despite of all exertion, I could not extricate myself. The men in the road considered me dead, and it was not till after some little time that one of them came out to set me free. Although my leg was not broken, I lost the use of it for the moment: I begged most urgently for a horse, offering gold upon gold, but men who called themselves my friends, forgot the word, and thought only of their own interest! I crept to the nearest house behind the front. An Englishman was charitable enough to catch a stray horse, place a saddle upon him, and help me up; I then rode again forward, when I learned that General Alten had been severely wounded. I saw that the part of the position, which our division had held, was only weakly and irregularly occupied. Scarce sensible, from the pain which I suffered, I rode straight to the hollow road, where I had left the rest of the men; but they also had been obliged to retire to the village in consequence of the total want of ammunition, hoping there to find some cartridges. A French dragoon finally drove me from the spot, and riding back, in the most bitter grief I met an officer, who gave me the above information of the battalion. I directed him to bring my men forward, if there were only two of them together, as I had hopes of getting some ammunition. Immediately after this, there arose throughout the whole line the cry of 'Victory!' 'Victory!' and with equal enthusiasm 'Forward!' 'Forward!' What an unexpected change! As I had no longer any men to command, I joined the 1st Hussars, and with them followed the enemy until dark, when I returned to the field of battle.

The division, which had suffered dreadfully, remained, during the night, on the field. Out of nearly 400 men, with which I commenced the battle, only 42 remained effective. Whoever I asked after, the answer was 'Killed', or 'Wounded'! I freely confess that tears came involuntarily into my eyes at this sad intelligence, and the many bitter feelings that seized upon me. I was awakened from these gloomy thoughts by my friend Major Shaw, Assistant Quartermaster General to our division. I felt myself exhausted to the greatest degree, and my leg was very painful. I lay down to sleep, with my friend, upon some straw which the men had collected together for us: on waking we found ourselves between a dead man and a dead horse! But I will pass over in silence the scene which the field of battle, with all its misery and grief, now presented.

We buried our dead friends and comrades; amongst the rest Colonel von Ompteda, the commander of the brigade, and many brave men. After some food was cooked, and the men had, in some measure, refreshed themselves, we broke up from the field to follow the enemy.

Return of the officers of the 2nd Light Battalion, two companies of the 1st Battalion, and the skirmishers of the 5th Line Battalion of the King's German Legion, who were present at the defence of the farm of La Haye Sainte, 18 June, 1815.

2ND LIGHT BATTALION

Majors

George Baring ....   A. Bösewiel..........Killed

Captains

E. Holtzermann......Taken prisoner   W. Schaumann ....Killed

Lieutenants

F. Kessler ....Wounded   T. Carey ....Wounded

C. Meyer ....   E. Biedermann.....

O. Lindam ....Wounded   D. Graeme...........Wounded

B. Riefkugel ....Wounded   S. Earl ....

A. Tobin..................Taken prisoner

Ensigns

F. von Roberston.....Killed   L. Baring ....

G. Frank ....Wounded   W. Smith ....

Lieutenant and Adjutant
   W. Timmann......Wounded

Surgeon G. Heise ...

1ST LIGHT BATTALION

Captains

Von Gilsa................Wounded   Von Marschalck...Killed

Lieutenant

Kuntze....................

Ensign

Baumgarten............

Skirmishers of the 5th Line Battalion

Captain
Von Wurmb............Killed

Lieutenants
Witte ....Wounded   Schläger.................

Ensign
Walther...................Wounded

Appendix 2

Major George Drumd. Graeme[*]
Inchbrakie, Crieff, December 6th, 1842

I fear my memory does not serve me so as to give you any material information on the subject, but I have endeavoured to the best of my power to answer your queries, which I return as they may be useful for you to see how far they are answered and shall feel happy if they are of the least use.

> Believe, &c.,
> George Drumd. Graeme

In the first attack I perceived *no* French cavalry on the British left of the farm of La Haye Sainte. I was favourably situated, and think I must have seen them had there been any, being placed with a section, of our Rifles behind the *abatis* across the high road a little in front of the great gate of the farm, afterwards with about a dozen men on the top of the *'piggery?'* (there was a calf in it!)

---

[*] Major General H.T. Siborne (ed.), *Waterloo Letters*, Greenhill Books: London, 1993, p. 406–9.

The [French] infantry came down in heavy columns with a line of skirmishers as thick almost as an advancing line of our troops. When close upon us we entered the farm, and closed the gates, and poured a constant fire on their Columns as they passed us, and even until they were up on the crest of the British position, when they were repulsed and broken by the British line, and repassed us like a flock of sheep, followed by the Life Guards, who came down the hollow road or sandpits, pursuing some French Cuirassiers (who, I presume, had been separated from their Regiment in the rear or to the right of our farm). A part our men sallied out and pursued in the crowd a considerable way up towards Belle Alliance. None passed *through* our *abatis,* as we afterwards returned, and I placed my men behind it as before.

The ground was literally covered with French killed and wounded, even to the astonishment of my oldest soldiers, who said they had never witnessed such a sight. The French wounded were calling out *'Vive l'Empereur.'* and I saw a poor fellow, lying with both his legs shattered, trying to destroy himself with his own sword, which I ordered my servant to take from him.

At this moment a curious circumstance occurred. Both Armies were quiet in their positions, and the Artillery had ceased firing, when we perceived a single French Cuirassier riding down the *chaussée* towards us. As he approached he waved with his sword, so that I said he must be a deserter, and would not allow my men to fire. He rode close up to the *abatis,* and raising himself in his stirrups as looking to see what was behind it, then wheeled round his horse, and galloped back to the French position, and in the hurry I believe the gallant fellow luckily escaped our shots which were sent after him.

The French came down obliquely towards the farm in the first attack, over the fields as well as down the high road. A large Column was all day in the rear [? front] of the farm, and trying to get possession of the barn, the door of which was open towards our right. They never tried to escalade, and we kept them off the great gate by firing from the piggery (where I was placed most of the day), although the *abatis* served them for cover, unfortunately.

I saw no *Sapeurs*. We had no loopholes excepting three great apertures, which we made with difficulty when we were told in the morning that we were to defend the farm. Our Pioneers had been sent to Hougoumont the evening before. We had no scaffolding, nor means of making any, having burnt the carts, &c. Our loopholes, if they may be thus termed, were on a level with the road on the outside, and later in the day the Enemy got possession of the one near the pond, and fired in upon us. This they also did during the first attack on the roadside.

. . .

I may add that the barn was filled with straw, and it was a fortunate circumstance that it was all carried off by the different troops during the night, the French repeatedly having tried during the attack to set it on fire. Lieut. Carey, in spite of the Enemy's fire, went out, and with his men, poured water on the flames.

Inchbrakie, Crieff, December 6th, 1842

Mrs. Graeme encloses a letter giving an account of the Battle of Waterloo, written by her husband with his left hand, then being at the age of eighteen; which may be interesting, as written at the moment; but which she requests may be carefully and speedily returned, as to her it is of considerable value.

Extract, June, 1815

We had all to pass through a narrow passage. We wanted to halt the men and make one more charge, but it was impossible; the fellows were firing down the passage. An Officer of our Company called to me, 'Take care' but I was too busy stopping the men, and answered, 'Never mind, let the blackguard fire.' He was about five yards off, and levelling his piece just at me, when this Officer stabbed him in the mouth and out through his neck; he fell immediately.

But now they flocked in; this Officer got two shots, and ran into a room, where he lay behind a bed all the time they had possession of the house; sometimes the room was full of them, and some wounded soldiers of ours who lay there and cried out 'pardon' were shot, the monsters saying, 'Take that for the fine defence you have made.'

An Officer and four men came first in; the Officer got me by the collar, and said to his men, *'C'est ce coquin.'* Immediately the fellows had their bayonets down, and made a dead stick at me, which I parried off with my sword, the Officer always running about and then coming to me again and shaking me by the collar; but they all looked so frightened and pale as ashes, I thought, 'You shan't keep me,' and I bolted off through the lobby; they fired two shots after me, and cried out *'Coquin,'* but did not follow me.

I rejoined the remnant of the Regiment, when we were immediately charged by Cuirassiers. All the Army was formed in squares. We hastily got our men into a hollow, and peppered them, so, I believe they found the cuirass not thick enough for rifles.

ENDNOTES

1 Bernhard Schwertfeger, *Geschichte der Königlich Deutschen Legion, 1803–1816*, 2 vols, Hanover, 1907, vol. 2, pp. 184–5.

2 Ludwig von Ompteda, *A Hanoverian-English Officer a Hundred Years Ago: Memoirs of Baron Ompteda*, trans. John Hill, London, 1892, p. 176.

3 Schwertfeger, vol. 1, pp. 61, 63.

4 Martin Howard, *Wellington's Doctors: The British Army Medical Services During the Napoleonic Wars*, Staplehurst, 2002, pp. 173–5

5 Sharpshooter detachments of the two light battalions had remained behind in Portugal when Sir John Moore advanced into Spain at the start of the Coruña campaign. They were still in the Peninsula in 1811, and rejoined the KGL Light Brigade at Campo Mayor on 21 June. North Ludlow Beamish, *History of the King's German Legion*, 2 vols, London, 1832, vol. 1, p. 189; vol. 2, p. 4.

6 Beamish, vol. 1, p. 333.

7 Sir Charles Oman, *A History of the Peninsular War*, 7 vols, 1902–30; reissued with two additional volumes, London, 1995–9, vol. 4, p. 287.

8 Guy Dempsey, *Albuera 1811: The Bloodiest Battle of the Peninsular War*, Barnsley, 2008, p. 274.

9 *The Times*, London, 12 January 1882. Obituary of J. O. Lindam.

10 Oman, *A History of the Peninsular War*, vol. 5, p. 597.

11 Oman, *A History of the Peninsular War*, vol. 5, p. 481.

12 Oman, *A History of the Peninsular War*, vol. 6, p. 425.

13 Beamish, vol. 2, p. 228.

14 Beamish, vol. 2, p. 440; Oman, *A History of the Peninsular War*, vol. 7, p. 537.

15 Alistair Nichols, *Wellington's Mongrel Regiment: A History of the Chasseurs Britanniques Regiment*, Staplehurst, 2005, pp. 142, 154, 175–7.
16 Oman, *A History of the Peninsular War*, vol. 7, p. 545.
17 Oman, *A History of the Peninsular War*, vol. 7, p. 505.
18 Oman, *A History of the Peninsular War*, vol. 7, p. 561.
19 Schwertfeger, vol. 1, p. 548.
20 Beamish, vol. 2, p. 364; William Siborne, *History of the Waterloo Campaign,* 3rd edn, 1848; reissued London, 1990, p. 294.
21 Schwertfeger, vol. 2, pp. 184–5, 188–9.
22 This narrative was first published in the *Hanoverian Military Journal*, part II, 1831, and is cited in Gareth Glover, *Letters from the Battle of Waterloo: The Unpublished Correspondence by Allied Officers from the Siborne Papers*, Greenhill Books: London, 2004, pp. 242–52

FURTHER READING

Anon, *Journal of an Officer in the King's German Legion, Comprising an Account of his Campaigns and Adventures in England, Ireland, Denmark, Portugal, Spain, Malta, Sicily, and Italy*, London, 1827.

Beamish, North Ludlow, *History of the King's German Legion*, 2 vols, London, 1832.

Bexhill Hanoverian Study Group, *The King's German Legion: From Bexhill to the Battle of Waterloo, A Story of the King's German Legion, 1804–1815*, Bexhill-on-Sea, 2003.

Chappell, Mike, *The King's German Legion (1) 1803–1812*, Oxford, 2000.

Chappell, Mike, *The King's German Legion (2) 1812–1816*, Oxford, 2000.

Coppens, Bernard and Patrice Courcelle, *La Haye Sainte, Waterloo, 1815: Les Carnets de la Campagne, no. 3*, Brussels, 2000.

Davis, Gwen (ed.), *The King's German Legion: Records and Research*, 2000; reissued Maidenhead, 2002.

—— (ed.), *The King's German Legion: Records and Research 2*, 2006.

Dempsey, Guy, *Albuera 1811: The Bloodiest Battle of the Peninsular War*, Barnsley, 2008.

Esdaile, Charles, *The Peninsular War*, London, 2002.

Glover, Michael, *Wellington as Military Commander*, London, 1968.

Gray, Daniel Savage, *The Services of the King's German Legion in the Army of the Duke of Wellington, 1809–1815*, Florida State University, 1970.

Haythornthwaite, Philip J., *The Armies of Wellington*, London, 1994.

Howard, Martin, *Wellington's Doctors: The British Army Medical Services During the Napoleonic Wars*, Staplehurst, 2002.

Longford, Elizabeth, *Wellington: The Years of the Sword*, London, 1969; reissued with its sequel (*Wellington: Pillar of State*) in 1992 as an abridged one-volume edition.

Muir, Rory, Robert Burnham, Howie Muir and Ron McGuigan, *Inside Wellington's Peninsular Army, 1808–1814*, Barnsley, 2006.

Nichols, Alistair, *Wellington's Mongrel Regiment: A History of the Chasseurs Britanniques Regiment*, Staplehurst, 2005.

Oman, Sir Charles, *A History of the Peninsular War*, 7 vols, 1902–30; reissued with two additional volumes London, 1995–9.

——— *Wellington's Army, 1809–1814*, 1913; reissued London, 1993.

von Ompteda, Ludwig, *A Hanoverian-English Officer a Hundred Years Ago: Memoirs of Baron Ompteda*, trans. John Hill, London, 1892.

Petre, Francis Loraine, *Napoleon's Conquest of Prussia, 1806*, London, 1907.

Pivka, Otto von, *The King's German Legion*, Reading, 1974.

Robertson, Ian C., *Wellington at War in the Peninsula, 1808–14: An Overview and Guide*, Barnsley, 2000.

Schaumann, August, *On the Road with Wellington: The Diary of a War Commissary*, trans. and ed. Anthony M. Ludovici, 1924; reissued London, 1999.

Schwertfeger, Bernhard, *Geschichte der Königlich Deutschen Legion, 1803–1816*, 2 vols, Hanover, 1907.

Siborne, Herbert Taylor, *The Waterloo Letters*, 1891; London, 1983.

Siborne, William, *History of the Waterloo Campaign*, 3rd edn 1848; reissued London, 1990.

Sprenger, Friedrich, *Geschichte der Stadt Hameln*, 2nd edn 1861; reissued Hanover, 1979.

Uffindell, Andrew, *On the Fields of Glory: The Battlefields of the 1815 Campaign*, 1996; reissued London, 2002.

Uffindell, Andrew, *The National Army Museum Book of Wellington's Armies*, London, 2003.

Vigors, D. D., *The Hanoverian Guelphic Medal of 1815: A Record of Hanoverian Bravery During the Napoleonic Wars*, Salisbury, 1981.

Weller, Jac, *Wellington in the Peninsula*, 1962; reissued London, 1992.

——— *On Wellington: The Duke and his Art of War*, ed. Andrew Uffindell, London, 1998.

Wheatley, Edmund, *The Wheatley Diary*, ed. Christopher Hibbert, London, 1964.

Wheeler, William, *The Letters of Private Wheeler, 1809–1828*, ed. Basil H. Liddell-Hart, London, 1951.

INDEX

Other books on the Napoleonic Wars published by
Frontline Books include:

1809 THUNDER ON THE DANUBE
Napoleon's Defeat of the Habsburgs
John H Gill
Volume I: Abensberg ISBN 978-1-84415-713-6
Volume II: Aspern ISBN 978-1-84832-510-4
Volume III: Wagram and Znaim (Publication 2010)

ISBN 978-1-84832-547-0

ALBUERA 1811
The Bloodiest Battle of the Peninsular War
Guy Dempsey
Foreword by Donald E Graves
ISBN 978-1-84832-499-2

THE WATERLOO ARCHIVE
Volume I: British Sources
Edited by Gareth Glover
ISBN 978-1-84832-540-1
Publication 2010

WELLINGTON'S HIGHLAND WARRIORS
From the Black Watch Mutiny to the Battle of Waterloo
Stuart Reid
ISBN 978-1-84832-557-9
Publication 2010

For more information on our other books, please visit
www.frontline-books.com. You can write to us at
info@frontline-books.com or at
47 Church Street, Barnsley, S. Yorkshire, S70 2AS.